# PARENTS:
# You've Got a lot To Give

*Edited by*
**Marie McIntyre**

AVE MARIA PRESS
Notre Dame, Indiana 46556

Library of Congress Catalog Card No. 72-83302

International Standard Book No. 0-87793-047-3

© 1972 by Ave Maria Press, Notre Dame, Indiana
All rights reserved

Photography: Cover, page 2, *Marne Breckensiek*
Page 16, *Patrick O'Malley*
Page 8, *Bryan Moss*
Pages 52, 82, 124, *Anthony Rowland*

Printed in the United States of America

# Contents

# Introduction

One of the big problems thoughtful parents and church educators face today is the reality that a great many Christians live their lives as though there were two worlds—a church world and a real world. These exist side by side and come together once a week, usually on Sunday or for religion classes.

This book has been prepared to help offset this false division and to help unify Christian education by concentrating on its primary environment—the home.

We've put together a series of articles by a variety of talented authors who would like to see the future generation live an integrated Christian life, seeing relationships, values, and everyday living experiences all related to and flowing from the central mystery of our faith—that we have a loving God who sends his Son to save us by making us free through his life and his Spirit.

We hope and pray that this little book, compiled from articles which first appeared in *The Parent Educator* and other booklets published by Twenty-Third Publications, will help readers to understand this unity and to promote it in themselves, their children and their friends and neighbors.

Marie McIntyre, Editor

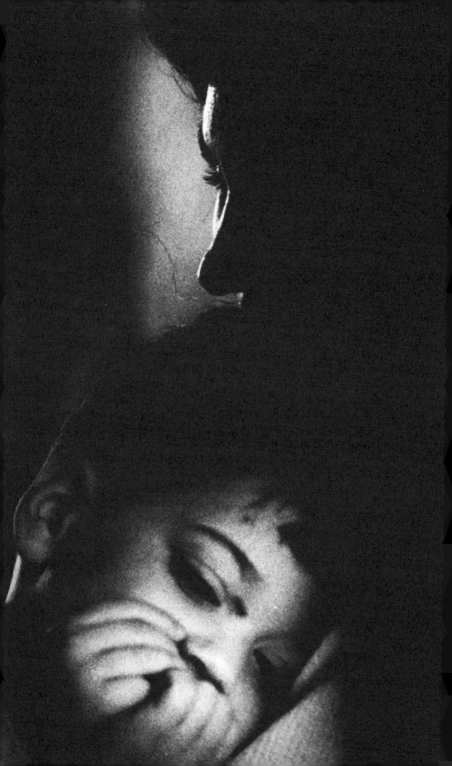

by Celia G. Scully

# 1. Parents:
# You've Got a Lot To Give

LABELING roles seems part and parcel of modern life. Unfortunately, the label does not always clarify the role. As Christian parents, you and I are familiar with our respective maternal and paternal roles, with our children's sibling and peer group roles, with our Church's teaching and sacramental roles.

However, since the Second Vatican Council, an old role has been tagged with a new label: We are "primary religious educators" of our children. Most of us still wonder what this means, and down deep, if it's really our thing?

"What do you do if you're not a teacher?" parents ask.

"They tell us we're primary religious educators, but it's like telling us we're the Church. Just try to make a suggestion or do something new. Then you find out the Church is still *theirs*!"

"The *Baltimore Catechism* was where we found our answers, but things are so different now. You've got liberal and conservative theologians who don't agree on sin, birth control, Mary, the Resurrection. How do you know who's right?"

You don't!

But the truth is one. Rather than facts or doctrine, it is a Person we must try to communicate—a Person no generation will ever understand totally. Differences of opinion are here to stay.

The real problem today is a parental crisis of confidence: What we "knew" once with certainty, we're not so sure we "know" now. Only more time, scholarly research, human experience, and the Holy Spirit will separate the wheat from the chaff of theological controversy. However, when we know Jesus personally, these matters become secondary to us.

We are not alone in a spiritual desert as long as we are open to the Spirit and willing to think. The buttoned-down mind is not compatible with Christian parenthood.

This means that parents, too, must be learners!

Where do we find the time? Our schedules are already overcrowded. So many things need doing in the house, the office, the volunteer organizations. We do serve Jesus in our brothers. Isn't that enough?

It depends on our idea of enough. As Christians we believe we live in a redeemed world, however imperfect. We live in an age of grace that happens to be a space age as well. We know God the Father as a loving and forgiving God because the man Jesus revealed it. This is good news, great news. Life is special. We laugh, we love, we celebrate. But one thing we cannot do: We cannot believe this *for* our children. Faith is not passed on like chromosomes. Each of us struggles with his own "I believe."

These days credibility and generation gaps rate big headlines. The role of mass media is being questioned seriously. World news is grim. The sexual revolution, drug scene, student unrest, war, racism, poverty, pollution—none of these escape us.

Often the radios, tapes, films, documentaries seem to reduce our role to that of mere listener or spectator. Man must also participate. Given a choice, we want participation to be peaceful rather than violent.

And so, we worry. The quality of life is important to us. We hope our children will make choices based on informed awareness. We share with other religions a vision of what man can become in order to fulfill his potential. We believe man is called to a love-relationship with God and, experientially, we have something unique to offer.

We have known love intimately. We have shared in the creative response of life-giving. The two things we know best are also two important attributes of God: He is a God of history who creates and he is a personal God who loves. At least we have a beginning and small beginnings should not be scorned!

The important thing is to go on from there. We can never exhaust the human dimensions of Jesus who during his life gradually revealed to us what God is like—the originating source of authentic interpersonal relationships.

Seen in this light, the problem for us becomes one of communication rather than lack of knowledge. And certainly the communication gap is not new. God sent the Word in person, for the prophets of old couldn't quite get the message across!

In the United States, getting the message across is a multimillion dollar industry. Just how great is the influence of mass media on concepts of meaning, values, religion? If our small children can barely distinguish commercials from the show, and our older children find "You've got a lot to live. Pepsi's got a lot to give" meaningful, then what is their level of gullibility or discernment? And further, if these slogans appeal and seem more like the "message" than the good news of Christianity, what then?

Then we must acknowledge the fact that mass media has introduced our children to a different world of learning, feeling, wanting—and start from there.

If we mean what we say, that God is omnipresent, that Jesus is *here,* then the greatest service we can render our children is showing them how to find God in contemporary places, persons, events. For this is the orientation of today's child. People, happenings, feelings, the present moment!

This, however, is not the way we learned to find God. For this approach to religion, we feel we are lacking necessary background, information, answers. The fact is that a real learning experience for the

whole family can occur under these very circumstances. And without heroic effort.

People still expect answers, verdicts, solutions.
But there is no Christian answering service. The bible
itself gives abstract principles and attitudes; Jesus
came to give us *life!*

Many attitudes contribute to acquiring an education
—secular and religious. Foremost is the realization
that education is ongoing. One learns all his life, not
necessarily in a formal way, and this makes life
fascinating. Essential are openness to new ideas,
willingness to consider different concepts, awareness
that a text is merely a beginning—still so much remains
unknown.

The present worldwide student revolt is forcing
us to reexamine the role of institutions of higher
learning. In the limelight as well are all other institutions—from family to government to church. In this age
of commercial and documentary, students are aware
(in a way that the Silent Generation was not) that they
are responsible for shaping and saving their future.

The role of the student himself is evolving. Learning
facts for themselves is not as important as knowing
where to find information, how to utilize it, how to
discover patterns and relationships, how to think.

The student is encouraged to question the known—
in order to learn to evaluate critically, explore options,
make assumptions, choose between alternatives,
respond to what is good (quality) and, ultimately, to
commit himself to action. Why is it so threatening
when he approaches religion with the same questioning
attitude?

Is it fear that we, too, will be questioned? Fear that
we will have to think in depth about our belief system?
Have we limited the Spirit only to comforting roles?

Also changing is the role of the teacher. No longer
must he, or indeed can he, have all the answers. The
continuing knowledge explosion is so vast that we all
share the role of learner.

The teacher is the "expert learner" who can provide materials for learning and organize the common search for knowledge. He (or she) knows how to learn, how to help others learn and express themselves, where to look for meanings and values.

He appreciates each child as an individual. The process of learning is of greater importance than the product. Thus, the teacher identifies with the student in the learning process. "This is where I am in my thinking," he says figuratively if not always literally, "and I would like to share it with you."

Substitute the word parent for teacher in the preceding paragraphs, and a good working definition of primary religious educator emerges. Parents may not be professional educators; but they can be expert learners.

What does this mean? What is this role that is described as "so decisive that scarcely anything can compensate for their (parents) failure in it"? (*Declaration on Christian Education*).

Basically, we are talking about a role that has sign value. The love, acceptance, forgiveness, and sharing which the child experiences are signs (which he does not consciously acknowledge) of the God he hears about. Our homes and relationships witness to what is important in our lives. Marshall McLuhan pinpoints the issue in these words: "Environments are not passive wrappings, but are rather, active processes which are invisible." Our values (good or bad, phony or honest) are not lost on the children—though it may be adolescence before they let us know!

Less obvious is the necessity of our providing the stimulus to learn more about God and showing that this learning is worthwhile. The home environment which we try to create must be one of love and honesty, so that each member of the family can know the Christ in freedom, as a basis for accepting or rejecting him.

First, let's face our limitations. The cultural, historical, theological heritage of Catholicism can be imparted to others. A personal commitment cannot. Faith is not forced. Jesus touched us in our freedom, and we must respect the freedom of others—especially that of our children. Often, the way to God the Father parallels the growth process of the adolescent toward his natural father—questioning, rebelling, thinking for himself. Have we, as well-meaning parents, set up pseudo-gods? Is spiritual growth possible in our family?

Second, what is it we want to communicate to our children as religion? Is it doing good? being good? having or believing something good? Precisely in this rethinking of what it means to be a contemporary Catholic and in Bonhoeffer's words, "who Christ is for us today," we commit ourselves to a program of self-education. Hopefully, as we know Jesus better, a new joy and freedom will enter our lives. Then our enthusiasm will be contagious.

Third, we must share the experience of working from *facts about* through *belief in* the person of Jesus. Theologians tell us Jesus was a fully mature person. Psychologists tell us there are definite stages through which each individual passes in developing the trust, autonomy, identity, commitment which characterize the mature personality. Thus parents, more experienced in the lifelong process of maturing, can share the learning process: how one "sees" with a Christian vision in an age which some describe as a collective "dark night of the soul" and others, the "dawning of the Age of Aquarius."

Practically speaking, this means getting out of old ruts of thinking, acting, worrying. It means abandoning the wishful thinking about "time to devote to religion" and realizing that religion and our lives as Christians are one. It means taking advantage of whatever will help us to understand people, culture, needs, and change—wherever they occur (and insisting our clergy do, too!).

It means an honest appraisal of our life style and

beginning afresh, if necessary. It means participating where we are. This may mean supporting good religious education programs or beginning in the least expected place—in our own homes, tailor-making a religious education program for the whole family.

Do we dare?

George Bernard Shaw once asked: "Must then a Christ perish in torment in every age to save those who have no imagination?" Lack of imagination—isn't this our problem as primary religious educators? We are afraid to experiment. Suppose we failed? Suppose our efforts differed from a neighbor's; who would be right?

Being a Christian has always involved risk. It has always involved love. Evaluating our experiments with an honest "This seems to help us love more; this doesn't," will make us more credible to our families, to our neighbors, even to ourselves. Gone are the paragons of virtue to be imitated. Instead, we become a community of believers sharing (not forcing) ideas.

Since the Spirit gives different gifts, it would be natural to find different experiments. Each family must search for a way which truly expresses its spirituality, its talents, its needs, its insights. Each family must have the courage to live with unanswered questions and yet continue the search for meaning in the words "I believe."

Imagination, courage, creativity—all are aspects of life style. Christianity, too, is a life style in which "personal growth is not optional for us. As a person able to think, each one of us must reach out towards the God who made him" (*Populorum Progressio*).

It is this reaching out, this relating to God and to man on our part which will make that "new tomorrow" a reality. Involved are much living, openness, loving—and ultimately, identifying with the suffering servant, Jesus.

When our role becomes our thing, then we *all* will be truly beautiful people!

# PART I

# Relationships in the Home

by Theresa Kopicky

# 2. Is Your Home An Orphanage?

"LOOK, mother, look at my rainbow." Five-year-old Philip Durran ran toward us on the patio. His mother and I were too busy discussing the condition of the world to stop and notice his rainbow. Mrs. Durran had supplied him with the soapy jar and the hoop but when wonders like making his very own rainbow had happened, we couldn't be bothered.

Suddenly this picture brought back to mind the days in the orphanage when I often wondered how the children on the outside lived. Discovering there isn't much difference between orphanages and normal homes, except for a frame of mind, I listed the things I missed most when I was inside.

First, there was the great longing for the out-stretched hand of physical affection. The gentle pat on the head, the touch of an arm or a hug, were the things we wanted desperately.

One of my friends told me she couldn't remember her father ever touching her either lovingly or as a punishment. "I would have welcomed even a spanking. At least I'd know he was aware of me."

Fathers are especially guilty and lacking in this respect. Somehow they seem to think it's silly or sissy to kiss or hug a child or shake an older boy's hand. Mothers too are sometimes forgetful. An example of this occurred when my husband and I went by to pick up our friends for the theater last week. The attractive mother of three was ready, except for the final instructions to the babysitter. Her little Joe came into the living room in his sleepers, not sure he liked the idea of his mom and dad leaving him. He climbed onto her lap and struggled to put his arms around her neck. "You're messing up my hair. Look what you're doing to my dress." She pushed him away.

What was little Joe's memory of that evening?

It's easy for us to say she should have gone into his room earlier and affectionately assured him, leaving him feeling secure before we got there. We can all tell others how to raise their children, but in my own family when the need for self-confidence, the second need, came up, we failed.

The second need was for someone to praise us, the need for self-confidence.

Our Mike proudly told his father, "I passed that history exam that I was studying for."

Dad was having his usual glass of sherry before dinner and wasn't thinking when he asked Mike, "What did you get?"

"C."

"You can do better than that." His father even spilled the sherry in his anger.

All the pride of passing was gone and an awkward silence was Mike's reply.

It's so obvious that tender loving care is the most essential need for all children to enable them to grow in spirit and develop. But I forgot that the evening when Linda, our oldest daughter, came home from school with plans for a surprise. She had learned to use a projector in school and after dinner she set up our projector, all ready to show home movies.

"What do you think you're doing with that expensive equipment? You're going to break it," I thoughtlessly scolded her.

That took the delight out of her surprise and she will remember that evening for a long time because her pride was stunted.

The third need in the orphanage was the longing for occasional privacy.

When this need was strongest, my little sister, Mary Ellen, found her own private hiding place in the musty cloakroom adjoining the study hall. All the coats were hung there on racks at designated places and the bottom rack coats touched the floor. Mary Ellen sat cross-legged underneath her buttoned coat, like an Indian. She squirmed with folded arms into the tent-like coat but her secret hiding place was discovered when we were all rounded up for our weekly dose of senna tea. It made no difference to Mary Ellen that everyone knew her hiding place because she returned to it time and again.

Consider our frame of mind in regard to privacy for our children. We take so much for granted and treat them like objects instead of people. We shout orders like sergeants. We'll put the "fear of God into them."

Fear makes a child timid and we have to begin again to bring back the self-confidence he needs for his own self-esteem.

A distressing point is that we fear so often what our friends or neighbors will think; instead we should worry what our children will think.

When Mike was 15, he saved enough money from delivering papers to get a jalopy to tinker on. When his father saw it he was upset: "What will the neighbors think of that heap of junk? Get rid of it."

I asked for a few days grace and Mike spent endless hours pleasurably tinkering. Some of Mike's friends became bored with their days and decided to run away from home. It was then his father was glad for the jalopy and didn't care what the neighbors might say.

Mary Ellen's daughter, Amy, was a clown in the school play. Her parents were mortified because "she's making a fool of herself." Instead of encouraging her creative ability and praising her courage, they let her down. It took a special something inside Amy to be able to get up on the stage to perform.

The fourth greatest need was having someone to listen to us.

In the dining room of the orphanage, we ate in silence, seated on wooden benches at long tables.

My gabbiness was often the reason for writing one hundred times, "I must not talk in the refectory."

At our home, I make up for it by talking at every meal but I must work hard at trying to listen, too.

There's a song that says, "People hearing without listening." How often are we such people, hearing without listening to our children? Granted, their problems are silly, but to a child the problems seem insurmountable. We must really listen and let them know we are listening. We should retain the vital interest needed but know when to stop asking questions and turn ourselves off. That's a large order.

My sister became a good bridge player and many afternoons she stayed too long at the tables. When she rushed home to prepare dinner for her family, time was very short. Her daughter leaned against her, weeping because the stitches in her 4-H apron weren't coming out even. "Can't you help me, Mommie?"

"What a crybaby. Instead of acting your age, you're acting like a baby." Stitches were far from my sister's mind when she pushed her daughter away with a motion of her hip.

When she told me about this later, I suggested it would have been easier to let Amy lean a little for comfort, with the promise of help after the meal.

Again, it's so easy to advise someone else but to forget when it happens in your own home. This occurred when the fifth need came up.

The fifth need is to develop friendships.

Children should be able to pick their own friends with some guidelines from the parents but without their parents degrading the friends for some peculiarity.

When Mike brought his new friend home to meet his family, a breach was created when we were too shocked at the friend's dirty bare feet to say "Hello."

Outsiders would think in an orphanage of 20 girls, friendships would be no problem. I don't remember having any good friends except my sister. Perhaps the chores and schoolwork kept us too busy. I remember feeling sorry for myself and Mary Ellen for being in the orphanage, but when the time came for us to leave, we both cried. Neither of us wanted to surrender the familiar for the frightening unknown. When we found a family willing to give us their outstretched hand, it bridged the gap of uncertainty.

Today, I'm happy to see that many orphanages have been replaced with foster homes, but it would be very sad to think the orphanage frame of mind has taken over in the home. We must not allow this to happen.

by Dorothy Dixon

# 3. The Importance of Affection

**M**R. GLENN was the policeman at the school crossing in our home town. Long past retirement age, and bedecked with a large white handlebar mustache, he was a living embodiment of gentleness and humor. Every day, rain or shine, he was there at the crossing, and every day he had a remark to set off guffaws of laughter as he directed the children across the street. Sometimes his humor was a little too true for comfort, but it helped us see ourselves as we really were. For me he always said, "Hello, raincoat, where's the little lady?" For, indeed, I was the smallest in my class and my raincoat was always so large on me that it obscured all but my hands and feet. For my friend Janie he always radiated a grin and called. "There's my friend 'Sour Pickles!' Come on, now, little one, let's have a smile." At that time, Janie would break forth in her first and probably only grin for the day. Indeed, Janie did give the impression of being "sour" and sad most of the time. Her face had a pinched and drawn look about it, and her eyes seldom revealed the healthy glow of childhood. It never occurred to me as a child to wonder what kept Janie so glum. Except with Mr. Glenn, she was perpetually blank-faced and listless. But now, from the perspective of time and psychology, I think back to her with a new understanding. I think of the times I went home with her after school. Janie's home was immaculately clean, and nothing was ever out of order. Her mother was always working diligently trying to have everything "just right" for her family.

But in all the days I spent in her home, I never once saw Janie's mother hug or kiss her daughter, or "pal" with her in any way. Janie had learned to keep out of the way of the mop and broom and to keep dirt off her dresses. But she had never learned to give and receive affection, for it was a missing link in her life.

Yet affection is almost as necessary for normal development as air and food. We say "almost" because a child can survive without affection, but the quality of the survival is bound to be seriously impaired. Although the capacity to love is inherent, the development of this capacity depends upon the circumstances of the life. A child cannot display outgoing affection and friendly attitudes until he has experienced them from someone else. The child who is sulky and withdrawn, or the child who is hostile and perpetually fighting, is, in most circumstances, the child who has not received the affectionate attention on which children thrive.

## How Affection Develops

During the first six months of life, a baby will respond to attention indiscriminately, in a generalized reaction of smiles and excitement of arms and legs. In the second six months of life, he forms attachments for the persons who are familiar to him, and who fondle him. Only in special instances will he show affectionate responses to strangers. Then the one-year-old becomes more skillful as he demonstrates his affection with hugs, kisses, and patting for the persons who have been closest to him and who have shown affection for him. Some schools of thought point out that this first expression of love is really an extension of self-love in that the child loves those who meet his needs. But there is no point in arguing which comes first: self-love or love of others. As normal maturing takes place, love that was once self-centered becomes outgoing, so that there is no limit to the kind of altruism that will eventually develop in a wholesome life.

The point that does need stress is that this maturing process is not automatic. Unless the child experiences love he cannot return love and grow to a wholesome maturity. Records of development in some orphanages tell tragic tales of children who have experienced little real affection, and their development lags markedly behind family-reared children not only in emotional and social growth, but intellectually too. Some of this emotional deprivation may be compensated for in later years when the children are placed in loving homes, but the amount of permanent damage that is done by extended deprivation of affection is inestimable.

Provided the child has had normal emotional nurturing however, further successive stages of development occur. At age two he may enjoy playing in the same room with others his age, though seldom will these children actually play together. They are too busy developing their own self-identities to enter into a give-and-take relationship with one another. But if, by the age of three, a child has developed enough confidence in himself, he may begin actually playing with, and thus relating to, his peers. Thus a certain amount of wholesome self-love is a prerequisite to the ability to share with others in a situation of mutual accord. But the daring it takes to relate to others is grounded in a secure relationship of mutual affection with the adults in the children's lives. By school age, these same children may not demonstrate as much overt affection to their parents as previously, but their love is just as real as ever, and finds expression in a growing companionship.

Thus we see that the development of outgoing love in children moves from response to parental affection through self-love to an eventual outgoing altruism. But the process is far from automatic, and it needs as careful nurture as do the physical and spiritual aspects of life.

## Love Among Brothers and Sisters

We often hear parents complain that their children "fight like cats and dogs." But actually this is not a serious complaint. Psychologists tell us that the siblings who contend the most often among themselves are the ones who have the deepest real affection for one another. When these same brothers and sisters are met with a common "enemy" from outside the family, they usually show strongest signs of mutual protectiveness. Also, the very fact that they contend among themselves indicates the degree of feeling they have for one another and thus the strength of their relationship. The fact that they feel free to express themselves openly with one another indicates a wholesome regard for one another.

Of course, bickering among siblings can go to unwholesome extremes. Parents who notice their children in a constant state of undue anger toward one another or who have reason to fear that one will actually harm another need to seek help, just as they would seek help in the case of illness. In fact, the family doctor is a good person to begin with in seeking professional advice in such matters. But complete silence between brothers and sisters is a warning sign to be taken just as seriously. It may be that the sibling who is unduly quiet has pent-up feelings or resentment that needs "airing" or talking through.

Sometimes there is a special alignment of brothers

or sisters, so that certain ones seem to "pair off" in a family. Such alignments are not usually lifelong, however, for interests shift as different stages are reached. When there are only two children in a family, these two may be especially devoted to each other. A few weeks ago, I attended a teachers' meeting in which we were asked to remember how we felt sometime during our tenth or 11th year of life. One lady, now in her 50's, recalled distinctly the anguish she felt the summer her only sister went away for a week to visit an aunt in the country. "It was as if my right arm had been amputated," the teacher recalled, "and I counted the minutes until my sister got back." Yet this person had been able to progress from this childhood closeness into an outgoing adolescence and a constructive maturity.

## Parent-Child Love

It is an unusual situation indeed when a parent does not readily respond to his child with affection and love. Aside from the fact that babies and infants are usually quite charming, these helpless creatures stir up the "need to be needed" in the adults who nurture them. The newborn humans enable their parents to fulfill their roles as father and mother, and the infants usually grow and become a lifelong source of satisfaction for themselves and for their families. The wise parent will enjoy his role as giver and receiver of affection, for the example of supreme parenthood is set for us in the eternal realm. We read in the Holy Scriptures: "See what love the Father has given us, that we should be called children of God: and so we are" (I Jn 3:1).

But just as our heavenly Father loves his children with steadfast love in spite of their shortcomings, so we as parents are called to love our children as they are. The temptation to love a child for what we

want him to be is a source of tragedy in many a life.
Some parents expect their children to win the same
honors they received in their childhood. But each new
life is unique and need not be patterned on a previous
one.

Other parents expect their children to make up
for something they themselves missed in childhood.
For instance, a parent who regrets not having violin
lessons may insist that her daughter become a "violin
virtuoso" even if the child shows no aptitude for this
ambition. In this case, it would be much more bene-
ficial for the mother to take the violin lessons herself,
even at that phase of her life, and let the daughter
pursue skills of her own. In any event, the love for
the child should not depend upon the performance
of the child, for such strains could produce disastrous
tensions.

Important as it is to love a child as he is, it is also
vital to help him become his better self. We show no
love for a child by ignoring his disruptive or self-
defeating ways. The words of Christ tell us: "Those
whom I love I reprove and chasten" (Rev 3:19). As
long as a child knows he is loved, he will thrive on
the kind of guidance, no matter how firm, that helps
him fulfill himself to his best potentialities. But it is
expecting more than a child can perform that does
damage.

Genuine love from a parent not only shows acceptance and guidance, but it also allows the child
gradually to gain independence. The physical closeness that characterizes the infant in the home is replaced by a companionate tenderness in childhood
years and by internal bonds of accord for later years.
The mother who has enjoyed her child's companionship through elementary school should have no
trouble letting him go away to summer camp during
scouting years and eventually to college in the late
teens. Parental love that is sound and lasting becomes
so internalized that it is not weakened by distance,

or time apart. It grows up with the child and does not need to remain under the same roof to be a lasting influence.

Whereas it is almost impossible to give too much affection to a child, it is quite possible, and unfortunately quite frequent in modern America, to give too many possessions to a child. Some parents are too busy with other activities of life to give much personal attention to their children, so they try to substitute material gifts. Thus we too often find children today surrounded by a roomful of toys but still wearing the sad, "sour" face of little Janie.

## Family Solidarity

Also important for emotional nurture in a family is accord between the various members. If the parents disagree on some phase of child rearing, they need to iron out their differences in private so as to present a consistent directive for the children. Children learn love from the examples their parents set. Differences of opinion are no disgrace, but mature handling of them can make the difference between a family of mature accord and a family of destructive bickering. Nothing is more harmful emotionally to a child than the confusion of differing sets of rules for him to try to follow.

But the family that works together is the family that grows together in the kind of love that has no end. After the struggles and triumphs of the years, there is no sweeter sound than the voice of the child pointing you out to a friend and saying proudly, "That's my mom and dad!" Such mutual elation is the fruit of love that is more than human. Indeed, real love is but an extension of the divine love poured into our lives, and characterized by the words of St. Paul:

"Love is patient and kind; love is not jealous or boastful; it is not arrogant or rude. Love does not

insist on its own way; it is not irritable or resentful;
it does not rejoice at wrong, but rejoices in the right.
Love bears all things, believes all things, hopes all
things, endures all things. . . . So faith, hope, love abide,
these three; but the greatest of these is love" (I
Cor 13:4-7; 13).

by Esther Kronenberger

# 4. Too Young to Understand?

**O**NE morning, when I was preoccupied with the terminal illness of my older sister, my daughter asked what was wrong. Sharply I blurted out, "Nothing, just leave me alone." But she didn't leave. There was something wrong. She just needed to know *what.*

Totally unsure that it was the right thing to do, I sat down with this innocent child, who had never seen death or the work of its cohorts, to explain that we would be bringing "Aunt Lur" home that day, she was still quite ill and could not live for too many days. God would take her soon, but, in the meantime, we would care for her. My child's only comment was that she would draw a pretty picture for her homecoming. "That will make her happy," she said.

What I anticipated to be frightening and depressing for her turned out to be a healthy experience for both of us. She merely accepted the truth, and left my side to busy herself in the inimitable fashion of a six-year-old, carefree and happy.

That was one of my first experiences in the need for honest discussion between my daughter and me. Since then I've learned that it is increasingly important that today's parents face the truth with children. We can no longer hide some of those unpleasant truths as we did in the past.

For example, how many parents remember the family's Aunt Grace who never married, who never left the upstairs back room? Neighbors knew Aunt Grace lived at home, but never questioned her whereabouts, nor asked about her health, nor invited her to any social or church functions. Aunt Grace was "odd."

The children knew of Aunt Grace too, but when they asked why she did nothing but cry in deep, sobbing groans or sit in a rocker day after day, they were quickly silenced. One day Aunt Grace was taken away. The children would not think of her again, the parents thought. But they were wrong. Aunt Grace was the topic of many silent thoughts and hushed conversations as they asked each other in fearful tones about the "Crazy House."

Today we are aware that one out of every ten people we know will at some time in his life suffer an emotional disturbance. Our children are taught that mental illness is no different or "worse" than any other disease, that it can be cured.

One friend I know who experienced a nervous breakdown attributes much of her recovery after hospitalization to the help of her three children. Many times during the day she would find herself sitting in a chair staring at nothing. When Stephen, her eight-year-old noticed, he would sit on the floor and hold her hand. In his quiet way he was saying, "I'm here, Mommy. Everything will be all right."

Ellen, the oldest daughter of ten, would brush her hair daily, remind her to apply lipstick, "so you'll look pretty, Mommy." She would help with dinner and the dishes without being asked. Even the four-year-old gave her strength by insisting she share his half-eaten apple or cookies throughout the day.

These children were told in simple terms of their mother's illness and needs and they responded in a natural, matter-of-fact fashion. The family situation gave them a feeling of belonging. They were never morose or frightened about their mother's condition.

Still, there are parents who, wishing to protect their youngsters, actually rob them of the opportunity to learn understanding and compassion. For too many

parents, mental illness and emotional problems still
hold that "crazy house" stigma of the past and children, regardless of age, are too young to understand.

That stigma also clings to the problem of alcoholism. Young people of another generation "knew"
about Father. He drank whiskey! But this was a
word they dared not use, nor could they ask why he
drank. The reeking odor was "cough syrup" or
"medicine" but Father never had a cold.

Standards of society branded him a drunkard
and eventually the children accepted the whispers
and taunts of their friends. "Your Dad's a drunk;
he's a bum." In some cases, he was given a one-way
ticket to the Big City to find his way with "his own
kind." In others, he was merely disowned by the
family, and children were told, "If you see him on the
street, just look the other way."

We've come a long way in facing alcoholism. Everyone knows of its shocking increase, yet too many parents today cannot, or will not, be honest in admitting
that it is the cause of their discord. Children already
know there's a problem but misconceptions of the
situation loom in their minds when the truth is kept
from them.

Jack, a classmate of my daughter, had an alcoholic
mother. When she lost interest in school or social
functions, Jack became a discipline problem and
eventually was suspended. Then he was readmitted
to school, obviously more stable and mature. A school
counselor, knowing the family problem, had encouraged Jack to join Alateen. It was through this
group that he was able to understand his mother's
problem and how it, in turn, caused his own crises.

Jack's mother is still an alcoholic, but now, at
least, he is capable of adjusting to it. This is a case of
society's taking over when the parent fails to be honest with his child.

Unpleasant facts are not easy to discuss, but even
happy truths have been kept from children on the

shaky premise, "they are too young to understand."
Take the subject of babies, for example. "Where did
Rita come from?" or "How did Joey get here?" were
asked in the past, but the answer was never a straight-
forward one, "From a most special place in Mother's
tummy." In some cases the new infant was simply
home when the older children arrived from school.
The question, "Where did he come from?" received a
variety of strange replies. "We just found him" or
"The doctor just left him" or "He was under the cabbage leaves."

In other instances, the new baby appeared after
much commotion during which the children were sent
away from the home. Imagine the terror and uncertainty that threatened the minds of the youngsters as
they were taken from their home. "Why do we have
to go?" "What's happening to Mama?" were questions that were never allowed a truthful response.

Even in these modern, sophisticated days there
are many parents who fail to share with their children
the absolute marvel of anticipating new life. True,
the question "Where did he come from?" doesn't
receive such ridiculous replies, but some are just as
unenlightening.

I was astonished at my own experience recently
with a mother and her teenage daughter. The girl, 15,
asked me to help one day when her mother was ill.
The woman did not have a healthy pregnancy and
events of the day included visits by her physician and
later an ambulance arrived for her hospitalization.

While leaving the house the doctor requested that
we locate the husband, asking that he go immediately
to the hospital. By then the girl was openly upset and
worried. "What's wrong with my mother?" "Will she
die?" "Why does my father have to rush to the hospital?" and "What will happen if we can't find him?"
were the questions she asked.

Assuming she already knew of the pregnancy, I
briefly explained that her mother lost the baby she was

carrying but that everything would be all right. As I predicted, everything did turn out all right. The mother was well and home within a week. However, the woman would not continue our friendship since, as she confided to another neighbor, I told her daughter a terrible thing—that she was going to have a baby!

This woman has seven children and I've wondered many times since then, "Where do her babies come from?" They have no cabbage patch.

These are the hidden problems which become most obvious, but there are countless others we tend to keep from children . . . father's shaky job, the financial worries, the marital problems, the religious doubts, the move to another city, the physical ailments, etc. It's important that young people see and learn how adult crises are met, how difficulties are solved. Many times they can be of much help in solving an unhappy situation.

While we do want our children to have a satisfying and happy childhood, hiding life's unpleasant or painful realities is not the answer. Our children do not need or want this type of protection. They want to know what is bothering us and they have a right to know. They are *not* too young to understand.

by Edna Maples

# 5. The Basic Need For Friendship

"IT kind of makes my insides rot. Here I am 11 years old, and nobody thinks anything of me. They think I am a piece of paper that they can burn and be left out of their lives forever.

"At noontime I sit alone, afraid to show my face to anyone because they might beat me up or make fun of me. Many people think I am dumb and stupid. When I play in a game they say to me, 'Get out of here, Gloria.' And when I am outside, they chase me away.

"I could cry out loud. Inside my throat is all choked up so tight I can hardly breathe. Sometimes I feel like I am in a deep well and I am frightened. I have tried to make friends, but at last they are gone too, just like my pride. My pride is nothing and never will be if the kids keep acting like this. As long as I can't have any friends, the world is pretty lonely.

"I'm not a dumbbell, and the kids who call me this know who I am and how cruel they are. I just wish they would stop. I won't sign this because the kids who tease me know who they are."

This is a copy of a note which was left in my mailbox at school. Imagine my consternation when I realized it was unsigned.

Being a school psychologist, I probably should be used to this type of reaction from children, but I'm not. This note left me sleepless for many hours during the following nights.

It was only after several attempts on her part that

this shy, frightened little girl made herself known to me. She came in after school one afternoon on the pretext of having lost a glove. Before I could respond to her query, she sobbed out her story of loneliness and unhappiness.

When I talked with her mother about it, she said, "I always thought it was best to let the kids work out friendships alone."

Hers is a common misconception. Parents do have a decided role in helping children make adjustments as they test methods of making friendships. They also have the right to ask, "How do I know when my child is having real trouble with others?"

Children always give clues to their feelings, regardless of the degree of seriousness. If a child is unhappy with someone, watch for him to be either negative and hostile or hurt and sad. He may come home from school and kick the dog, slam a door, or just plain be angry with his family. If queried, he may blurt out, "Bobby doesn't like me." If Bobby is his best friend, his mother knows there has been a big, big disagreement and that this is a temporary barrier.

Consolation may not help at this time. He doesn't want to hear a lecture or even to be reminded that his trouble is probably temporary. He neither wants anyone to be on Bobby's side nor to say anything bad about him. The most help he can receive at the moment might be to say, "I know you are upset and hurt with Bobby today. Is there anything I can do to help you feel better?"

Just accepting his feelings as normal may be enough, but offering aid will let him know someone cares what happens to his friendships. If he makes no suggestions, drop the matter for he probably is already on the way to reestablishing his contacts. Children seldom carry grudges and, depending upon the age and sophistication, reestablish contacts without embarrassment. In other words, the past is forgotten and the present is another day, with new worlds to conquer.

Take the girl who wrote the note above, for example. Once her mother and I began working with her, she changed over a period of time. She is not the same today. She is becoming a leader in her fifth-grade class and is very much accepted by her peers.

How do I know this? I received another note in my mailbox recently, and it was signed. It reads: "You were right about the kids in my class — at least, some of them. I have some friends now; maybe because I'm a better friend, like you said. Before, I was afraid of the boys and girls in my class for fear they wouldn't like me. They thought I was stuck up and didn't want to be their friend. Like you said, I was shy. School is nice now."

This episode made me wonder about other children in our school and their experiences and feelings regarding friendships. As a result of this curiosity, I talked with many of the children and received some interesting comments about their views.

Jann, a fourth-grader, said, "A real friend is someone you can trust."

Tommy, a seventh-grade student, took a different approach. He said, "To make a friend you must have something in common, otherwise it won't develop. You just have to wait and see."

Tommy went on to explain that he is basically a shy person and that he really is afraid to attempt friendships. He said, "I'm afraid to approach others because of fear of rejection." There is, however, a ray of hope already breaking through since he is an excellent pianist and is overcoming his shyness through performing. He is being accepted by his peers because of his willingness to play for some of their social activities.

Adults may be taking a great deal for granted when they assume that children have no problems making friends. Few people I know are concerned with this seemingly big problem many children face almost daily. How can children be concerned about school performance when there are other, more important problems to consider?

Denise, a first-grader described a friend as, "Someone who will play with me." Six-year-old Robert described his best friend as: "He lets me use his crayons and eraser and plays with me on the playground. He sometimes pushes me in the swing." These children are interested in immediate gratification — a what can you do for or with me? It is rather a cause-and-effect relationship—you do something for me and I'll like you best.

These friendships can be short-lived as these children are merely seeking playmates. They are compatible one minute and are feuding the next. Usually there are no grudges held over for the next day, or even the next few minutes. They lose their tempers, but are ready to return to their play activity in a very few minutes. Unless, of course, there is adult intervention with all its connotations and innuendos.

A fourth-grade boy, Dan, says of his best friend, "He likes to do the same things I like to do. I find him with a good personality. He doesn't mind if I joke about him. He likes to make others happy and to laugh. He laughs with you."

Janet, another fourth-grader, said, "My friend is nice to me. She is friendly and talks with me. She plays with me and is fun. We are more than friends at school. She plays with me at home too."

These students seem more perceptive and are better able to verbalize feelings involving others. They are more revealing of their own personalities yet still like pupils who are nice to them. It became rather evident at this point in the research that the maturity level of these students was showing. I could hardly wait to encounter some of the older students to get their reactions.

Vickie, a sixth-grade girl says of her best friend, "She is always friendly and fun loving, always smiling. We are friends out of school too. We go to the games together and to town shopping." Her counterpart, Galen, described his friendship with another boy by saying, "He invites me to everything and we come to school together. He comes to my house and plays with me. He also shares things with me."

These students seem more mature in their judgments and make their selections more on social performances. They appear to do more analyzing of character traits.

In a group guidance class where I was involved, a group of fifth-grade girls decided that friends need not have the same skin color, be of the same religion, or be physically fit. One girl related a story about a friend who is a deaf mute. She found a way to communicate with the girl so that they are now close friends.

Everyone needs to belong to a group or have a close friend. The child who is on the outside or on the fringe of a group is usually unhappy. He often becomes a discipline problem because of the hostility generated toward the rejecting group or individuals in the group. It stands to reason that a child is happier in school and attempts to keep up with the class if other children accept him.

The descriptions of friendships as expressed by these children are very refreshing. There was no one who expressed an adult viewpoint of prejudice and misunderstanding. Even the child who was crushed internally made an excellent adjustment when she found the tools to solve her problem.

If parents have tried to help and problems still persist, perhaps a visit to the teacher will help establish a path to pursue. The teacher will have definite knowledge of students and their interaction and will be an ally in maintaining situations to resolve problems.

In this time of great mobility, parents can create

an atmosphere of acceptance in the home which will help children through times of distress. The children will adjust to their loss of friendships and make others easily if parents understand their needs.

Sometimes the simplest message is the best hidden. It takes a perceptive parent to sense unhappiness in a child, but rooting out the cause and going to work to eliminate it might be the wisest use of parents' time. After all, when one member of the family is unhappy, the whole family senses it. It's up to the whole family to prevent it.

by Anne Tansey

# 6. Criticism Cripples Kids

"**H**OW do you keep Larry at home so much?" a neighbor asked the mother of a teen-aged boy, adding, "My Jim never stays home."

"We don't keep Larry at home," the boy's mother responded, "he comes and goes as he chooses, but he evidently likes to be at home."

When Larry's mother repeated the conversation to her husband he asked, "Why didn't you tell her the truth? She never stops criticizing Jim and his father is even worse."

The night before Jim had complained forlornly, "I think my father hates me. He doesn't like my hair, nor the way I walk, nor the clothes I wear and yells about my report card even when it isn't bad at all."

Parents who criticize their children consistently fail to realize that they are waging a cold war in their own homes, rearing barriers between themselves and their children, creating the much-talked-of communications gap between the generations. Children do not want to stay around parents who are always carping at them. As one boy expressed it, "It's like never knowing when you are going to get stung by a bee."

This enemy of the home and family is sending more and more children into the streets where there are more and more temptations for them to get into trouble. Many parents with problem children do not realize that they are the cause of the delinquency of their children.

Not all children go into the streets and get into trouble, but many are being injured psychologically and socially. "It's like all the lights go out when your parents say they are ashamed of you," one girl told a school counselor. Parents do not seem to realize that children can be hurt by the things they say to them in criticism. In some cases chronic criticism is a habit which parents fall into. In other instances the parents unconsciously work off their own tensions and frustrations onto the children.

Constructive criticism has its place in the home if it is actually constructive and properly applied. One can scarcely rear children without counseling. However, counseling and destructive criticism are poles apart and each has an entirely different effect upon the child.

Some children rebel against parental criticism, others are crushed by it, some lose confidence in themselves, others develop nervous habits. The home is the last place a child with a critical parent wants to be. Adults do not want to live in an unhappy home but children are compelled to do so. No one wants to be in the company of anyone who is always criticizing them and sitting in judgment upon them. This is human nature.

There is usually a reason why a person, parent or otherwise, is a chronic critic of a particular individual. It is important for the carping person to find out why he or she can find nothing but fault with the one toward whom he feels antagonistic when others do not share their convictions or negative judgment on the person. A teacher disagreed sharply with a mother who claimed her child had certain faults which the instructor had never seen displayed. "Perhaps you are seeing what isn't there," she told the mother firmly.

Parents oftentimes use parental concern as a cloak for their antagonisms for certain children. In one instance it may be that the child resembles a relative whom the carping parent doesn't like and that dislike is projected to the innocent child. One husband was considerably disturbed by the critical attitude of his wife toward one of their daughters. He could not reconcile his wife's criticisms with his own observations.

The man had often heard his wife express intense dislike for a certain aunt whom he had never met as she lived in a different city. While on a business trip to the city he stopped by to see the aunt and was struck by the resemblance she bore to the daughter his wife was so hard on. In that moment he understood.

In some cases a parent sees in a son or daughter a fault which he or she possesses and loathes. When that same fault is manifested by the child they use a heavy hand upon the child to break the fault. I have never ceased to be amazed at how hard a heavy drinker can be on another person who drinks. It is as though a guilty person cleanses himself by condemning another.

There is also the matter of jealousy. One woman could not understand why she could never find anything good to say about her sister, until she faced herself squarely and admitted she was jealous of the sister's beautiful home and economic security. Once she did that she never again had any desire to criticize her sister.

This is as true with parents as with relatives and associates. In one instance a professional counselor made a father realize that he was jealous of his son because the boy had an intellect superior to his. The father saw the son breezing through school with very little effort whereas he had been forced to study hard to make a passing grade. As a result of this unsuspected jealousy he had precipitated a crisis in the family which demanded outside help.

A good deal of trouble between some mothers and their teen-aged daughters is caused by jealousy. A mother may find herself both diminishing in looks and sex life and be unconsciously envious of the girl ready to embark on the adventure of life. Many mothers refuse to accept such a supposition, yet in their excessive criticism of their daughters they give every indication of this to others.

The same is true of fathers and sons. It is not unusual to see tensions arise in the home when boys and girls vie for the attention of spouses. These possibilities cannot be overlooked. The sooner they are recognized and confronted the sooner the cold war between parents and children melts with love and understanding.

by Kenneth Heiting

# 7. Effective Discipline

**M**OST of us don't give much thought to the whys and wherefores of discipline until trouble comes—trouble in the form of a disobedient son or daughter. Perhaps Johnny doesn't ask for permission to go down the block, maybe Laura stays out later than she should. When this happens we usually punish our children in order to impress upon them the fact that they must do as they are told. This usually works—next time Johnny remembers to ask for permission, and Laura watches the time more carefully.

But sometimes our message goes unheard, sometimes our children fail to obey in spite of repeated warnings. This often leads us to try one type of punishment and then another as we search for something that will "work." But what if we're not successful, what if we don't find the answer? Should we forget about the issue? Should we be more firm? Should we resort to physical punishment?

These questions can be answered when we look at what we mean by discipline. What are we trying to accomplish when we discipline our son or daughter? Generally speaking, we are interested in educating or training them to become adequate and self-sufficient adults. Although we usually associate punishment with discipline, closer examination reveals that this is not the main factor. The central concepts in discipline are education and training, not punishment.

Children learn how to behave by watching us; psychologists call this the process of identification.

For example, you've probably noticed how a little girl will talk of growing up and "being like mommy." She has seen her mother go grocery shopping, cook meals and take care of the baby and she wants to do the same. A boy will often talk of being like his father. Just as our children want to be like us in terms of career or employment, so they naturally take after us in the ways that we behave.

If that's the case, does it mean that children who misbehave have bad parents? Not at all. What sometimes happens is that in the closeness of family living things become "sticky" and family members are unable to see the situation as it really is. Such mix-ups can occur in any family. To straighten things out, to see the situation more clearly, family members need to objectify their relationships with one another.

We can objectify our relationships with our children by talking things over with someone we trust. It is generally better to talk with someone outside the family since our marriage partner is as close as we are to our children. A neighbor, a friend or a relative may be helpful. We should keep in mind, however, that since these people value our friendship they may not be completely objective; they may be reluctant to say anything that we will not like to hear. But, in spite of this liability, friends and neighbors can often give us helpful advice on minor, everyday problems. If more serious difficulties arise, it is usually best to go directly to someone who has had professional training in counseling and child guidance. School social workers, guidance counselors and psychologists are usually consulted when serious behavior problems arise.

Experts in the field of mental health have a number of suggestions to help us more effectively raise our children. For example, psychologists who have studied parent-child relationships have discovered that the most effective means of modifying behavior is to use what is called positive reinforcement. An example of this is a mother who praises her youngster for brushing his teeth. The opposite of this is negative reinforcement—punishing a child when he does not do as he is told. Studies have shown that positive reinforcement—praise—is more effective with children than punishment.

Sometimes, however, our children are not receptive to approval or praise. When this happens we need to use punishments in order to help them behave appropriately. However, we should be careful not to overpunish or underpunish, but rather try to have the punishment fit the child's misbehavior.

For example, when Susan is late for supper the second night in a row and she does not have a valid excuse, her parents may get their message across by serving the food that is now cold and not allowing her to have any dessert. Susan's parents may underpunish if they merely scold her; they may overpunish if they deny her desserts for a month. The idea of what is the right amount of punishment cannot be stated in general terms; it depends upon each individual child and set of circumstances.

Studies prove that discipline is most effective if administered as soon as possible after a child has misbehaved. Such an approach is particularly important with young children since they have short memories. Keeping this in mind, mothers do best to handle punishments themselves rather than warning children to "wait until your father comes home."

Studies on child behavior have also shown that it does not matter so much whether parents tend to be firm or lenient; rather, the important factor is that both parents agree on the disciplinary approach. When parents disagree and openly argue about strictness and leniency there is a likelihood that their children will be adversely affected.

Every family has its own way of handling punishments. As each child grows we begin to sort out various punishments, finding which ones work best with each child. Perhaps five minutes in his room works well with Bobby, while only stern words are needed with Carol. It is generally recommended that physical discipline, such as spanking, be used sparingly and only with young children; once a child begins grade school it is best to use other disciplinary techniques.

When the usual disciplinary measure does not "work," we often resort to many different tactics in order to control our youngster's behavior. First, we withhold this week's allowance; later, we deny him a trip to grandmother's with the family; finally, in desperation, we take away a chance to attend the prom. What do the experts recommend in such cases?

There are some things in a child's life that should be placed beyond the realm of punishment. In other words, a child should know that there are some things which he will always have or will always be able to do no matter how he behaves. This tells him that we love him no matter what happens. Many counselors recommend that children receive an allowance every week, without fail. They also suggest that children be allowed to travel or go visiting when the family does so as a group.

In addition, they indicate that there are some things in the life of a child that should not be denied—graduation exercises, birthday celebrations, family outings, etc. Psychologists emphasize that fun times are important in every child's life, as is the knowledge that he is accepted and loved by his family.

While this may sound like we should always behave in relation to our children's needs, such is not the case. Sometimes we need to curtail a youngster's behavior not for his benefit, but for ours.

A mother's recent experience illustrates this point. When the Allen family's dog died, their four-year-old son, Jimmy, was quite upset and didn't want to be left alone. He was constantly underfoot, asking questions and wanting his mother to play with him; Mrs.

Allen found that as the days passed he was getting on her nerves. Although she knew that Jimmy needed her, she also felt that she needed a break, some time away from him. She decided to make arrangements for a babysitter to take Jimmy for a walk every morning. When Jimmy refused to go with the babysitter the first morning, Mrs. Allen was in a bind. Should she give in to Jimmy's wishes or should she demand that he go with the babysitter? Since Jimmy's pleadings suggested that he was quite distraught, Mrs. Allen gave in to him.

Was this the best solution? Probably not, since Mrs. Allen is expecting too much of herself; she should have sent Jimmy off with the babysitter for a few hours each day. Such a break would have given her a chance to revitalize her emotional state so that she would have been better able to cope with Jimmy for the rest of the day. In other words, parents do have the right to occasionally place their needs ahead of their children's; there are times when parents come first.

It sometimes happens that after we discipline our son or daughter we feel a need to change the punishment. Let's say, for example, that Tom Jones comes home from a Saturday date an hour later than he is supposed to. Mr. Jones is quite upset and tells Tom that he cannot use his motor bike for a month. The next day Mr. Jones begins to feel that perhaps he has overpunished Tom. It isn't that his son is complaining about the imposed discipline; rather, Mr. Jones has begun to feel that being an hour late should not equal a month's denial of the motor bike.

Is it all right for Mr. Jones to change his mind and lessen the punishment? Consistency is said to be important with children; would changing the punishment make Mr. Jones inconsistent? Child psychologists tell us that in such a situation Mr. Jones should feel free to shorten the punishment since this alternative is being considered not because of pressure from Tom, but because of Mr. Jones' assessment of the situation.

Mr. Jones should explain to his son that he feels he made a mistake and that he has now decided to shorten the punishment. In a way it is good for Tom to see that his father makes mistakes and that making mistakes isn't such a terrible thing after all. Psychologists tell us that children are painfully aware of their many mistakes and shortcomings. They often see their parents as perfect, or nearly so, and feel that they will probably never make it to adulthood because of their own imperfections. It is comforting for them to see that they don't have to be perfect as they grow up.

Child specialists suggest that parents occasionally examine the disciplinary techniques that they are using. Parents can ask themselves such questions as: Do we emphasize punishments too much with Johnny? Is Gary too old to be spanked? Can we find ways to praise Linda more often? Periodical examination of disciplinary techniques can lead parents to be more effective in raising their children.

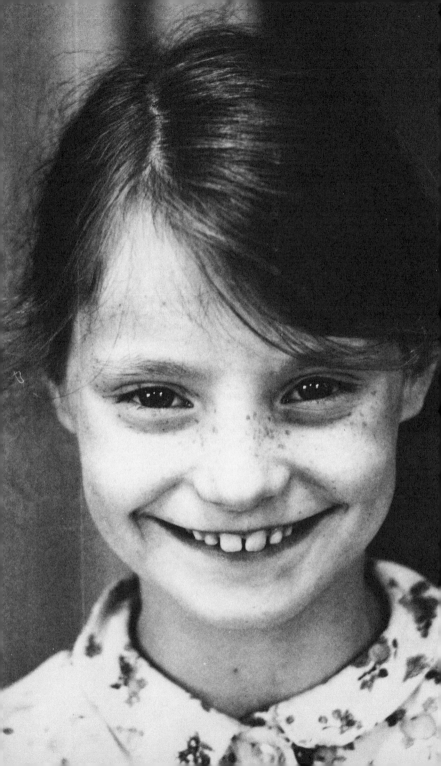

# PART II

## Religious Education in the Home

by Edmund Curley

# 8. The Family Bible

EVERY year the national best-seller lists carry the bible in a top position. Of course, the rating is an honorary one. The bible is not as widely read or influential as we would like to think it is—especially, sadly so, in Catholic families.

There are many reasons why large numbers of Catholics are not yet "at home" with the scriptures. Not so many years ago scripture reading was actively discouraged by the Church's leaders and educators for any but the formally trained in theology. The "Modernism" scare and the following official clamp-down on unrestricted bible reading by "the faithful" did much toward causing the condition in this country. On a global Church level it is a fairly old malady—going back to the Protestant Reformation and the official Church's fears of personal interpretation of dogma.

Thankfully, this is no longer the case but the ill effects linger. One of the regrettable consequences is the lack of bible reading in Catholic homes and, in far too many cases, total absence of the holy books. By bible, incidentally, I mean the *whole* bible, Old and New Testaments—the complete recounting of salvation history.

As far as families are concerned, the bible should be *the* book. After all, it is the family story in the highest degree, the absorbing and inspired tale of God's family—mankind. It is the history of God's loving concern (*hesed*) for all his sons and daughters down through the centuries.

In this regard, the bible contains all the elements of a family history:

The origins of the family are there, in Genesis for example, and especially in the story of our spiritual forefather, Abraham, who went out alone to listen to the call of God and thus set the scene for acceptance of the covenant that would determine all Hebrew history to follow.

The maze of relationships and chronologies that make up any family's lengthy story are there, too, as are the family's high points, sorrows, joys, and triumphs. It is an honest history with fully as much emphasis on familial shortcomings (e.g., treasonable worship of idols in the desert) as to victories where the family courageously clings to faith and overcomes adversity.

Most importantly, the bible as a history of God's family is thoroughly suffused with hope. Hope is everywhere—in God's promise to Adam and Eve, in the eyes of Abraham when told to sacrifice his son, in Moses' heart, in David's resolution before Goliath, in Solomon's dreams for Israel, in all the prophets, all through the pages of the Old Testament culminating in Jesus' words for us, his followers. Hope is the essential ingredient of family life; it begins with the early love of a man and woman, grows changing through years of child rearing, and continues with the family's growth and maturation. Hope, the central theme of the bible, follows this family parallel.

There are many things a family needs—from mutual respectful love to some degree of financial security. The bible is an acute requirement, for nowhere else is our spiritual heritage so intensely present as in its pages. If there were no bible to read, to ponder, to meditate upon and learn from, the core of our spiritual life would be missing. The bible is for our Christian belief what the soul is for our personhood. It is at the heart of things. It is not a good book to have around; it is an essential for Christian (family) life.

Bring the bible back as *the* family book. If you have a copy, take it out of the bookcase; if you don't own one, get one and while you are about it, pick up a plastic cover at the local dime store. Cover the book with this plastic or oilcloth and then leave it around. The bible certainly belongs on your kitchen table as much as *Better Homes* or *Joy of Cooking.* It need not take second place in the living room to *Time* or *National Geographic.* And it is certainly just as apt for bedroom reading as *Redbook* or *Argosy.* If it seems out of place in any room, the fault is not with the bible but with our society's view of where it belongs.

In addition to leaving the bible in an available spot, use the opportunities for reading it which occur naturally. Tie it in to "teachable moments" whether they be the quiet time of a serious family discussion, preparation for a religious holiday, or just a time when "the air is right." Lent, Advent, and the days immediately before major holy days are obvious times, but you will find many more proper to your family when you begin to look around.

It is a good idea to mark appropriate sections, chapters or verses that apply specifically to your family's birthdays, anniversaries, and other important moments. Sometime when you have a few spare moments, go through the Psalms or perhaps Proverbs to find sections with the best appeal.

Regular readings are always effective; the family that has established a set time will find the other suggestions very easy to adopt. Setting aside ten or 15 minutes every evening for a reading period sounds simple enough but, frankly, in these hectic times this may often be impossible. If this is the case with your family and a strain results from such an attempt, it would be best to try an easier approach, a less regular one at first.

If you want to involve your children in bible readings, don't hesitate to begin with the most exciting or emotionally appealing sections. It is always a good idea to read the chosen verses over first so that you can simplify complicated phraseology for younger boys and girls. There is nothing wrong with choosing deliberately exciting sections and then simplifying the wordings of these.

More and more reading experts are telling us that a child's enthusiasm for books can best be stimulated by providing him early with texts he can *enjoy.* The same is true with the bible. And don't worry about continuity. Pick the most engrossing parts for kids— the stories and people with whom they can identify: Noah, Jonah, Samson, David, Jesus as he cures the lepers, raises the little girl, etc. Let the children identify and lose themselves in these tales. You may be giving them piecemeal selections but, like their faith and ours, the bigger picture will develop later.

Above all, don't succumb to the parental danger of worrying so much about doing it right that you end up not doing it at all.

When all is said and done, this boils down to one piece of advice: Start reading the bible now. And don't forget that plastic cover.

by William Ann Maloney, OLVM

# 9. Help Your Child Appreciate Baptism

**W**HEN you help your child to appreciate baptism, you have a lesson at once so interesting, important and tremendous that finding ways and means of making the pages of the lesson "come alive" for the child are very important. Despite what the Pepsi ad would tell you, you really come alive the day of your baptism. The title of the lesson in your children's religion text could well be: "God made me his child."

The best way to initiate your child into a gradual understanding of what it means to be a baptized person, is to help him recall what it means to be a member of his own family. What makes him special and different from the other children who live on the same street? Why is his name different? What does it mean to be a son or daughter in a family? What are the signs that "we belong"? What do we do together as a family? After the answers are thought through and expressed, the child will be ready to listen to your revelation about his life as a member of God's family which began in a special way, at his baptism.

The day your child became a child of God, deep inside, the power for a lifelong transformation process began. He now lives with the life of the Father. He is now a member of God's family on earth, the Church. He can claim the great God of heaven and earth as his Father, Jesus as his elder brother, and Mary as his mother. He belongs to a noble family; he is rich with all the wealth of his heavenly Father at his disposal.

Explain to your child that when he was baptized, God his Father called him personally to become his son. God acted in his life just as surely as he did in the lives of the holy people of old, such as Abraham, the apostles, the prophets.

The best way, then, to teach your child about the wonderful meeting that took place at his baptism is to start by celebrating his baptismal day, and likewise to make it a point to celebrate each baptismal day in the family.

You will want to celebrate this special day just as you would a birthday. You can place his baptismal candle on the table by his place. You may not have the child's original candle, but you can get a blessed candle and decorate it somewhat like the paschal candle. Explain it simply, even to the younger ones. Tell them that the candle reminds them of Christ, the light of the world who, in baptism, gave them a share in his own life. Just as Jesus by his actions and words helped people to be happy and to love, so we are to do the same. A candle gives light. We give "light" too, by our going out to people to brighten their lives.

Once in a while, before the child goes to bed, have him draw a picture of how he let his "candlelight" shine during that day. Hang up the picture. You could replace it with different pictures that he makes from time to time, all of which will show him how one lets the Christ life shine forth.

Discuss with your child or with the whole family at a meal, the meaning and the many uses of water. Bring out how water gives life, purifies, makes things grow, gives joy, and also how it can destroy. You can see in this very brief summary how you can make the application to the water used in baptism.

Then, if at all possible, take your child to witness a baptism. Explain the various meanings of the ceremony. It is helpful to point out that at baptism we enter into an agreement with God to become his son and to please him by acting like a son of a loving father. As the child grows older, encourage him to renew the promises made on the day of his baptism. This deepens his consciousness of the loving father-son relationship he has with God.

Another good practice and one that could be a part of every baptismal celebration is that of making a card or drawing of the various items used in the baptismal ceremony. Send the card to the godparents, thus teaching the child to remember that the god-parents are a very important part of the ceremony.

Sometimes overlooked is the fact that the members of the Christian community assume a certain respon-sibility for the welfare of the baptized. The godparents are the ones chosen to represent the community and they are to aid the child whenever needed. The main duty of both parents and godparents to the newly baptized, it would seem, is to limit the power of evil as far as possible in the child's life by providing the child with a thoroughly Christian environment.

Some of the stories from sacred scripture that you may want to relate to your child to help explain baptism are: the story of the Exodus of the holy people of God from the land of Egypt (Ex 14:1-29). Here your child will see God at work saving his people through the waters of the Reed Sea. Still another story of value for this lesson is the event when Jesus is talking to the Samaritan woman at the well (Jn 4:1-30). Also, the story of Nicodemus, the Jewish ruler who came to Jesus at night, is important. Jesus gives Nicodemus an explanation of baptism that we cannot afford to over-look (Jn 3:1-21).

You will not want to miss any of those events from scripture that ring out loudly and clearly the wonderful works of God. It is wise to remember that these lessons should unfold gradually in the life of your child as he, too, like Jesus, advances in "age and wisdom and grace."

by William Ann Maloney, OLVM

# 10. Lead Your Children To The Eucharist

**P**ARENTS who help their children to share the parish family meal at the table of the Lord find that this is a thrilling and sublime task which also deepens their own personal appreciation of this gift of God's only begotten Son.

The happiness and closeness that a child feels at the family meal are basic before he begins to experience this new meal and larger family eating at the table of the Lord. He has begun, as it were, in the words of the psalmist, to "taste and see the goodness of the Lord."

All through history, a meal has always had special meaning and significance. It is interesting to note that here and now in the late 20th century, the meaning of the meal is basically the same. For example, when funds were needed to finance the campaign for the late Robert Kennedy, what did his friends do to raise funds? They planned a series of dinners to testify to the esteem and respect they all shared for him. Likewise, it was an opportunity for those who were united in their loyalty and esteem to share something of their own joy and sorrow, and this they could do naturally as they shared a meal.

When we stop to consider the coffee break so common in our own day, we can see that this habit, too, is designed to foster a time to share ideas and grow in friendship. In the same way, many a contract has been signed and many a sale made as the salesman and his client shared a meal. It would seem that as man shares a meal, he shares something of himself.

Why not get a photo album and have the children make their own book for first Communion? As you tell the stories from scripture that show the sacredness and holiness of a meal in the lives of the people of God, you will want to have your children make a picture of the event. You will also want them to print a few words that convey the meaning of the event taking place in the pictures that they have drawn. Remember that God always uses very common every-day things and events to make himself known. In this case, it might well be this booklet that you and your child are making together.

Once you have grasped the message that the bible story holds for your child, it will be easy to help him make the booklet. Your child might find it easier to make the picture with stickmen or, again, he might want to trace something and color it. Letting him express it in his own way is important.

Suppose you choose Genesis 18:1-15 as the basis of one of your lessons. You will point out the kindness and politeness of Abraham to the visitors. When Abraham saw them coming, he asked Sarah to prepare them some dinner. He wanted to share something with them. God showed him how much he loved him, because as Abraham shared this meal with his visitors, they gave him a very important message. They told him that God would send him a son. God often speaks to us as we share a meal with one another. God is very near to us when we eat together and listen to what he tells us through father and mother and the rest of the family. (Later, it will not be difficult for the child to see how natural it is that God speaks to us in the epistle and gospel readings at the eucharistic celebration.)

You could have him draw a picture of Abraham and the visitors and another picture of his own family eating together. You could guide him to put a few words of explanation over each picture. For example, one might be, "God shares a meal with Abraham."

The one over the picture of the child eating with his family might be a short, spontaneous meal prayer such as "God bless us and be near us as we eat together."

The next lesson that you could teach is found in Exodus 16:1-36. As you tell the story, you will highlight the gratitude and joy that the hungry Israelites must have felt as they gathered the manna that God so lovingly provided each day. God is still feeding his holy people today on the living bread that comes down from heaven, and this living bread is the body of Christ that we receive each time we go to Holy Communion.

The two pictures that would emerge after you have told the story would be one of the Israelites gathering the manna. The message over this picture could be: "God feeds his people on their way to the promised land." The other picture would be one of the child going to Holy Communion. Over this the caption could be, "God feeds us living bread on our way to heaven." Under these pictures you might suggest the words from the Our Father, the family meal prayer recited at every Mass, "Give us this day our daily bread."

Another story to help deepen your child's understanding of God sharing a meal would be the one found in John 6:1-15. It is the one of the multiplication of the loaves and fishes. Here, we would want to point out the great love and concern that Jesus had for the people. Today, at Mass, Jesus feeds us his own body and blood. He gives himself to us. The message over the picture of Jesus feeding the multitude could be, "Jesus gives life-giving food to the five thousand." Over the other picture the wording could be, "Jesus gives himself to us as the bread of life."

The most important part of this story takes place the next day. The people go out the next morning to find Jesus. They want to make him king, so that he will always give them food. It is at this time that Jesus makes them a wonderful promise to give them his own self to be their food. Many of the people did not believe

Jesus and went away (Jn 6:66). Let your child decide on a suitable picture around the theme of John 6:51: "I am the living bread that comes down from heaven."

These stories have led the child to the tremendous and sublime event of that first Holy Thursday night. Before the child can appreciate the fact that Christ was celebrating the Passover, the central event in the lives of the Israelites, he must be told the story of the first Passover as found in Exodus. After that, tell the story of the Last Supper. You might want to relate it as you find it in Luke 22:1-20. This, too, the child can illustrate and print the simple words of consecration. Explain that it is at this meal that we gather to make our offering to God and to celebrate with joy his goodness to us. This helps us to remember how we are related to God in and through Jesus.

These are the key lessons that your child will want to know before he receives the Eucharist for the first time. They can be taught very naturally and simply as you share a story from scripture with your child. The greatest challenge to many parents today is to provide times of silence and recollection in the home. In such an atmosphere, deep pondering about the mystery of the Eucharist takes place. It is for this reason that we have suggested times of drawing when the child can be silent and recall the event you have narrated. He will learn to treasure the booklet he has made and also he will come to treasure the memory of you as you led him to the table of the Lord.

by Mary Perkins Ryan

# 11. Our Children, Ourselves, And Confession

CHILDREN will gather from observing when their parents go to confession, and their attitudes before and afterwards, the meaning this sacrament has in their lives and its value in helping them make new beginnings as Christians.

However, when a child has reached a stage at which private confession might be helpful for him, parents might explain the meaning and value it has for them, and might have for him, in terms suited to his understanding. If he then wants to go to confession, they might direct him to a priest who could best assist his moral growth. Above all, parents can give their children a warm confidence in the unfailing mercy of God and in the assurance of this mercy that one receives in the sacrament of penance.

One difficult problem is that faced by parents whose children have already been trained in the "how many times did you commit what sin?" approach to sin and confession. How best to help them to an approach that will more effectively inspire and guide their moral and spiritual development depends, of course, on their age and on the intensity with which they have "bought" or rejected the approach they were trained in.

With adolescents, however, it would usually seem advisable at some point to say quite frankly, "We allowed you to be trained this way because this was the way we were trained. We now realize that we belong to a growing, changing Church, and we are trying to grow with it and hope that you will want to too. Let's try to sort all this out as well as we can together."

## About the Sacrament

The development of the sacrament of penance has had a very complicated history; both the rite and its role in the life of individuals and the church community have changed over the centuries, and a great deal of rethinking of both is going on today.

In any case, as the Church has traditionally taught, God's forgiveness may come to us in many ways. All these ways depend on our own "conversion," or contrition. We must turn to God in sorrow for our sins, opening ourselves to his gift of forgiving love, which is always there, waiting for our acceptance. Within the Christian community, various rites provide us with signs of our conversion meeting with God's forgiveness. The penitential rite at the beginning of Mass is one such sign. Penance services are another. But the sacrament of penance is the full and formal sign of reconciliation with God and the Christian community and, as such, it has a very real role in Catholic life.

## Why Confess?

The Church's traditional rules on when we should go to confession stated two things. First, that those who are sure in their conscience that they have committed mortal sin should go to confession before they receive the Eucharist. Second, that those who are conscious of mortal sin should go to confession at least within the year. These two rules, obviously, take account of the fact that mortal sins may already be forgiven in some other way. However, they insist on the need for the formal sacramental sign of reconciliation with the worshiping community of the Church.

It would seem to be much more difficult to commit a mortal sin than most of us used to believe. But certainly, if anyone is conscious that he has intentionally directed the whole thrust of his life away from the love of God and of his fellowmen, and wishes to turn back to love again, he should seek the formal sacramental sign of forgiveness and reconciliation.

Again, in our moral development, many of us come to realize clearly, now and again, that we have been unloving and have acted unlovingly in some area of our lives. We experience a "conversion," and feel the need to make a new start. At such times, it would seem most appropriate to go to confession.

Further, as we have seen, the actual guilt which we bear before God and our brothers may get very mixed up in our emotions with leftover immature guilt-feelings that originated in our childhood. When we realize that there is something seriously wrong with the direction of our life, then, our sense of guilt and failure may leave us very confused and uncertain. We may waste a lot of time and emotion in anxiety about whether we have committed a mortal sin or not. Going to confession, and simply telling the priest how mixed up we feel and what a burden of failure we are carrying, may not only give us a calm assurance of God's forgiveness, but help us get started again much more quickly and purposefully on our task of loving and caring.

Again, we all experience times when guilt and failure become a burden that begins to cripple us a little. We need some visible sign of love, of hope, of reassurance. The formal character of God's forgiving word uttered personally to us by the priest in confession helps us experience effectively what we know in theory—that God loves us still and is calling us into a fellowship of care with our brothers.

Then, too, our taking part in communal prayers for forgiveness may sometimes not seem to reach some very personal problem in our lives. These are occasions when we might well go to confession to seek God's mercy and peace and, perhaps, the advice of an older brother in the faith.

Finally, many of the people who have been going regularly to confession for many years feel that doing so has been a source of growth, a wonderful gift of hope and peace. Even though going to confession frequently no longer seems so much to be what all devout Catholics do, such people should have no hesitation in continuing a practice which is still helping them grow.

Again, no one should have any hesitation about trying to find a confessor who he feels will be understanding and meet his particular needs. In fact, traditional moral teaching indicates that any obligation to go to confession is conditional on a suitable confessor being available. We need to remember that confession is a human dialogue between two persons, as well as an effective sign of God's loving pardon. People are right, then, in looking for a priest who will understand their point of view and help them understand God's message of hope and pardon. However, if a person is really looking for counseling over some complex personal problem, it is usually better to approach some understanding priest outside confession and arrange for an ordinary interview.

All in all, then, while many of us may not go to confession every week or every month, as we used to do, when we do go we would hope to make it a less routine and more serious sign of some kind of "conversion." We would hope to have it lead to a real "celebration," however personal and private, of God's forgiving love becoming actual in our lives and of our recommitment to that love and its demands.

# 12. Confirmation: What Is It All About?

**A** FEW years ago in a Dublin theater, a man sang in front of a large audience. The audience thundered its applause as he completed selections from famous operas. Then he sang "Mother Machree" with such tenderness that it was soon obvious that this song was meant for someone in the audience. That someone with silver hair and a wrinkled face and the chapped hands that had worked so hard to put him on the stage sat silently with tears running unashamedly down her face. She understood the message in his song. And, of course, the people noticed it too, and other eyes were misty before the song ended.

We can get caught up in the emotion of this scene because we have lived such experiences. Many centuries ago, another man had a lived experience that has even a greater message than the son singing to his mother. This man was, in a sense, all of us talking about the Father of all of us.

It happened in Nazareth, the home of his childhood. St. Luke tells us about it: "On the Sabbath, he went according to his custom to the synagogue and stood up to read. A scroll of the prophet Isaiah was handed him and, after unrolling the scroll, he came upon the place where the following text occurs: 'The Spirit of the Lord rests upon me, because he has anointed me. He has appointed me a messenger to bring the good news to the humble, to announce release to captives, and recovery of sight to the blind, to set the oppressed at liberty, to proclaim a year of grace ordained by the Lord.' "

Before the day was over, if Luke isn't combining three different events in this story, this man received not applause but threats and an attempt on his life! Yet, when we read the passage he quoted from Isaiah and the statement he made following it—that this was being fulfilled that very day—we can find here a great deal of help to understand the mystery of our confirmation.

God's Spirit, anointing, appointing to a saving task to help those in need are all mentioned in this episode. When we take a look at confirmation, we discover all these elements are also present.

We can look to the common element of confirmation and discover that a meditation on the hidden meanings of oil can help us to appreciate the meaning of confirmation. Here again we are aware that as human beings, we learn through our senses and that God consistently uses sensible signs and events to communicate with us.

The fact that God chose such common elements through which to reveal his love for man is a marvel of simplicity. Water, oil, bread, wine—all of these necessary-for-life materials, have much to say to us about God's love, and about life. Even in our culture, a child emerges from a watery womb and is massaged with oil. Oil has a function that "continues and strengthens" life, as it were. Let's take a longer look at it.

When you ask a neighbor, "What does oil say to you?" you probably get a blank stare and a raised eyebrow. If you ask, "How many uses and values can you think of for oil?" you immediately set his mind spinning over the possibilities.

Oil is used for fuel. It gives energy in order to get a thing done. Oil is needed for power. Oil is a source of strength. Athletes rub oil into their muscles to limber them up so that they can achieve a victory. Oil gives us heat which is necessary for the continuation of life. Oil gives light and people who grew up without electricity know how precious this is and how alive things become when the darkness is dispersed and light floods a space to give the opportunity to work and learn.

Oil is associated with smoothness, with pleasantness and when it is scented as in cosmetics, it makes its presence known in a delightful way. Oil preserves things and keeps things from getting rusty, useless. Oil has healing powers to restore lost health and strength.

We could say much more and so could you and your neighbor, but keeping these characteristics of oil in mind, let's see what all this has to do with confirmation.

The matter used in the sacrament of confirmation is holy chrism—a scented or perfumed olive oil. It is mixed with balsam and consecrated by the bishop (on Holy Thursday) who uses a prayer which includes the plea that those who are given the Spirit of Christ may "be permeated through and through with his royal, priestly, and prophetic honor and clothed with the robe that is the gift of incorruption."

This prayer refers to the threefold function of Christ which becomes ours at our baptism and is deepened in our confirmation: king, priest, and prophet.

What does all this really mean to us? We've been confirmed. How do our children learn the meaning of what this sacrament signifies in our lives?

Well, when we go back to the bible to search for precise statements about confirmation, we don't find anything that clearly says that the apostles confirmed by using holy chrism. In fact, the evidence is that the action involved was the imposition of hands with prayer. For example, we can read about this in Acts 8: 14-17: "Now when the apostles in Jerusalem heard that Samaria had accepted the word of God, they sent Peter and John to them. On their arrival they prayed for the Samaritans, that they might receive the Holy Spirit. As yet he had not come on any of them,

because they had only been baptized in the name
of the Lord Jesus. Then Peter and John laid their
hands on them, and they received the Holy Spirit."
Also, we see the same in Acts 19:2-3, where Paul is
talking with some disciples at Ephesus: "Did you," he
asked them, "receive the Holy Spirit when you became
believers?" They replied, "We have not even heard
that there is a Holy Spirit." "What kind of baptism
then did you receive?" asked Paul. They replied,
"John's." "John baptized the people," Paul answered,
"with a baptism of repentance, telling them to believe
in him who was to come after him, that is, in Jesus."
On hearing this they were baptized in the name of
the Lord Jesus, and when Paul laid his hands on them,
the Holy Spirit came on them, and they began to speak
in tongues and to prophesy.

The laying on of hands signifies a personal communication—a contact that imparts power from one
person to another. In the sacrament, it symbolizes
the imparting of divine power, the Holy Spirit's grace.

Notice that baptism and the imposition of hands
follow each other, and notice, too, that the placing of
hands on the forehead of the one to be confirmed is
part of the external sign of confirmation.

Although the gospels, the Acts or the epistles
do not tell us that Jesus or his followers used perfumed
oil to call down the Holy Spirit, there is a strong
biblical basis for the significance of anointing.

In the Old Testament, kings, priests and prophets
were anointed, the former with oil, the latter with the
unction of the Holy Spirit. The Messiah who was to
come was to be the Lord's Anointed. That is what
"Christ" means: The Anointed One. *Christos* is simply
the Greek translation of the Hebrew word *messiah*
which means the Lord's anointed. And we know that
Christ was not anointed with oil, but with the Spirit.

So, in Christ, with the threefold function of priest,
prophet and king, the early Christians saw the totality
of holiness, and they began to use the word anoint

when they meant to make holy, to set aside for God. By the fourth century, we have quite a bit of historical evidence that Christians were using oil along with the imposition of hands to indicate the significance of confirmation. But the first Christians already understood that to be a Christian meant to be as much like Christ as possible—to be holy, which meant to be set aside, to be consecrated to God. That is why they understood that they were the anointed of God, because they were in Christ. St. Paul was so aware of this that he wrote it to the new Christians at Corinth in his second letter to them, Cor. 1:21, 22: "It is God who has established us firmly along with you in communion with Christ and has anointed us and stamped us with his seal, and given us the Spirit as the first installment of what is to come."

Paul knew that the people he spoke to had a long tradition of understanding the meaning of anointing. (Paul would have the same hard time religion teachers have now if he tried to explain this to our generation.) Prior to coming to Christ, the people understood that anointing had the following principal effects:

1) Consecrating a person to God

2) Showing that God had chosen this person to do a special task

3) That the Spirit of Yahweh (God) was conferred on him.

The important thing, then, is that anointing is symbolic of a mission, of being given a task to do, a work for God. Those who are anointed are to show forth the power of God in whatever state in life they are. In the Old Testament, this was usually priest, prophet, or king. As Jesus is all these in one, and we are baptized into Jesus, we share not only his sonship but his mission, which is this threefold task of serving the world as priest, prophet and king. We are anointed so that we can give witness to who we are—members of his body, set apart to be a light for others, to show forth the truth and to speak it (to be what we say we are)—the role of a prophet; to worship the Father as sons—the role of a priest; to lead others and guide them—to bring order into areas where there is a disorder in society—the role of a ruler or king.

This all boils down to the marvelous fact that when we were baptized we were *Christ*ened. When we are confirmed, we are commissioned to share our sonship with the world. We are no longer children of our Father only, just receiving and living comfortably at home. As someone put it, "Once confirmed, we can never go back to Nazareth and settle down." We have a task to do, and God gives us help to do it.

St. Peter reminds us of this and when we read Peter's words in his first epistle, 5:10-11, we can't help but think of the characteristics of oil which we talked about earlier. Peter says, "God, the source of all grace, who has called you to his eternal glory in Christ, will himself, after you have suffered a little while, perfect, steady, strengthen, and firmly establish you. To him belongs power forever and ever. Amen."

Now, before we go on, it might be good to stop and think about what we are trying to do. Here we are in the 1970 decade far removed from the culture out of which came the symbols and meanings that tell us so much about the meaning of confirmation. Yet, even though many of the externals do not mean any-thing to us, we can look around and become aware that the inner meanings remain. For example, instead of thinking with the thought patterns of an early Christian, let's look at a drop of perfumed oil (chrism) and see what it says to us in our own words and in our own times and culture.

Here are a few hints of the meaning and value of oil and every one of them can be transferred to our task as confirmed Christians. Let's think about them slowly and meditatively, make the connection and apply it in our own lives:

Oil speaks of heat . . . light . . . warmth . . . strength . . . comfort . . . healing . . . power . . . suppleness . . . ease in movement . . . giving life . . . penetrating . . . unifying . . . sealing . . . preserving . . . clinging . . . abiding . . . remaining . . . what else?

As the oil of our anointing in confirmation is perfumed with balsam, we can ask, too, about the properties of perfume and what this tells us about our confirmation:

Perfume speaks of welcome . . . delight . . . gladness . . . joy . . . sweetness . . . praise . . . charm . . . persuasion . . . attraction . . . pleasant presence . . . preciousness. Perfume is diffusive of itself, like goodness, like virtue. It makes both its subject and its object special and different, set apart from its surroundings and environment. It speaks of sharing . . . it mingles . . . it draws together in the very act of spreading out . . . it permeates . . . it clings . . . it changes or modifies that to which it clings . . . it transforms. What else?

From all the thinking we have just done, we can come to a deeper understanding of what it means to be confirmed, to be anointed and sealed in our consecration to God in Christ and given a share in his mission through the presence and power of the Holy Spirit.

We have not explored every facet of confirmation here. We have just tried to look at it through a study of the outward sign used—the anointing with chrism. We haven't even talked about another of the outward signs—the imposition of hands and the passing on of the power of the Spirit given to the whole Church.

But, nevertheless, now when we go back to read with Jesus what St. Luke records in 4:16, we realize that what our Lord said of the words of Isaiah, "This day this prophecy is fulfilled," also applies to us: "The Spirit of the Lord rests upon me because he has anointed me. He has appointed me a messenger to bring the good news to the humble, to announce release to captives, and recovery of sight to the blind, to set the oppressed at liberty, to proclaim a year of grace ordained by the Lord."

Confirmation gives us the Spirit in a new way— to proclaim, to bring people to freedom in many ways. Our job is to go out to people, like traveling salesmen, and share our wares by making their presence known and by the witness of our appreciation of them. Gratitude and joy, like perfume, can leave their presence felt for a long time and influence the lives of others. The spirit of confirmation will be shared with our children not so much by what we teach them explicitly but by how we live implicitly. Then they will know why it is both a joyful and a responsible thing to be sealed in his Spirit and be aglow with his life—a life lived for others.

by Marie McIntyre

# 13. Our Task As Christians

As soon as we, as parents or as individuals, quietly face the fact that the evils in the world are too big for us to tackle alone, we become aware of the need for more strength and power to accomplish the feat of making any significant advance in the defeat of the forces of disintegration and alienation in our world. We become aware that we must be part of a group or a team using all the resources, talents and powers that are available to do our job.

This is just one reason why there is so much stress today on the need for community—not organization, but community—a group of people united by a common awareness of a task to be accomplished. The astronauts were a community. So are apostolic teams doing parish work. So is a basketball team with co-operating rather than competing players. So are some religious congregations, particularly in small cluster-of-interest-and-work groups. So are loving families.

But how does the man who works a full day and comes home tired at night, content to drink beer and watch TV, become a committed Christian? How does the woman with a houseful of children become an obviously confirmed Christian when she has no energy left at the end of a giving day? How does the pre-teen, teen, and post-teen show the world that being confirmed in Christ makes a real difference in their lives when they are so busy with school activities and allied interests?

Is this a false question? I think so.

Our mental images of what Christianity means indicate the kind of training we have had, the kind of presuppositions we have taken for granted, and the kind of culture patterns that have influenced our thought patterns and the values we accept as good and true. Isn't it true that many of us associate Christian activity with something specifically related to working "in and for the Church"? Preaching, teaching or sup·porting the Catholic school, promoting CCD classes, doing work in church-related organizations to raise money, promoting aid for the disadvantaged, etc.— these are the activities that come to most minds when we ask what actions in their lives are specifically Christian. Ordinary, everyday work is rarely mentioned and yet, it is here that most people spend their lives producing goods and services to make this world a better place to live in, and influencing others for better or for worse in their daily work-world contacts.

What is a Christian called to do in this world-of-church, world-of-world tension? Do we opt for one and forget the other? That would be to judge that our choice is right and anyone who opts for the other is wrong. The current polarization between groups which stress one portion of revelation in opposition to another helps us to see that selecting part of the whole of life does not lead to healing and a witness to true understanding.

Is it possible that a Christian is not called upon to perform a specific work which we have come to call "holy"? Is it possible that a Christian is one who is called to believe and to surrender to the God who demands this surrendering response to his love which we show the world by witness and by service? This means that Christians are people who express in their everyday lives their awareness that they have been saved in Christ and are willing to carry on his saving work by "being there" for anyone who needs them. There is no running away from this-*now*-world in order to

reach the kingdom of heaven. As Jesus cried out to be
delivered from the death of the cross, but faced it
for the sake of us, his brothers, we confirmed Christians
are called on to cry out against the crosses of evil,
but may not run away from them. We take them up
too—in their many obvious and subtle forms. It is not
the work itself that makes us different from the non-
believer who battles evil—we can be on the same
team working together on this—it is our understanding
and belief that salvation is an ongoing process and
as Christ moved through his 24-hour cycle witnessing
his Father's love and serving others who needed
him, we are called to be this witness and this servant
to our present time.

What is most needed, then, is not a list of "apostolic" activities in which one can become temporarily
involved to feel that he is contributing to the cause,
but an awareness that confirmed Christians cannot run
away, cannot come down from the cross, and cannot
melt into the apathetic masses who are unconcerned
about the ongoing redemption man needs.

The man who drinks his beer in front of TV at night
has a right to the kind of recreation he needs and is
no less a Christian for being human. The woman
whose day is filled with services to the next generation
must not feel guilty if she cannot muster the strength
to attend nightly meetings at the parish hall. So many
church-related meetings are called to convince
people that they are not being Christian enough. Yet,
if we would understand in gratitude, our salvation-in-
serving wherever we are, such meetings would have
little purpose.

The world which is America is rich with opportunity
for confirmed Christians to witness their belief in
Jesus as Lord and Savior, and to serve men by helping them overcome prejudice based on ignorance,
hunger based on unjust poverty, fear born of misunderstanding, greed due to selfishness and nonbelief,
boredom caused by dehumanizing jobs and oppor-

tunities, loneliness caused by man's unconcern, love-lessness because we are not loving enough.

We will always have the tension between the "yet and the not yet," between the "being and becoming," between those who believe that the Church is not of this world and those who believe it cannot be anything but of this world, between those who express the insight of the Spirit and those who strive to maintain the kind of law and order that keeps all people in the same mold. St. Paul's epistles are full of the recognition of this. This is the given situation which we must face and work through, striving to love, reconcile, and understand people who take different views. Taking sides is not the answer, not when the task is one of unifying, healing, reconciling, atoning.

We are in a world already on the threshold of breaking into a new kind of civilization with patterns of behavior and values very different from the ones we have inherited. This is not new in the history of the Church, nor is the pattern of resistance by the former generations' establishment. What is new now is the availability of instant communication and the acceleration of gradual evolution into what appears to be revolution. The times now and ahead call for Christians with the willingness to move against injustices and evils in every form with a prudence that might be labeled imprudence, but nevertheless a difficult search for the best way to operate in order to heal rather than cause further disintegration.

Who can spell out what these forms should be? Some laws will be broken because they do not bind the genuinely concerned Christian or they need to be headlined so that we will see the need to change them for the common good. The most important thing is that the law that needs to be kept—the law of love—demands that we be truly willing to lay down our lives for our friends. This usually begins at home where our closest neighbors—our family—live. This means daily service which witnesses to our belief that "he who loses his life will save it." This is what the resurrection is all about. This is why Jesus is Lord and King, and knowing this, we who are Christians, know that there is no other answer. Jesus is . . . yesterday, today and forever.

# PART III

# Special Concerns in the Home

by Edna Maples

# 14. Emancipating Your Children

"**W**HEN can I begin to trust Roger to make the right decisions? He is so easily led into trouble by the boy next door."

This question came from the mother of a kindergarten child as she sat in one of our parent discussion groups at school. She directed the question to me, the school psychologist, but before I could respond other mothers entered the discussion and posed some questions.

"Why don't you forbid him to play next door?"

"Why don't you talk with the boy's mother?"

"Why don't you have the children play in your yard so you can watch them?"

"Why don't you talk with Roger?"

"Why don't you have your husband do something about the boy next door?"

"Why don't you punish Roger?"

This episode took me back to a parent conference a few days earlier—a conference much more depressing. I listened to Jerry's mother sob as she told me how her 18-year-old son had flunked out of college his first year because he was unprepared to meet and solve several situations which arose soon after his arrival at school.

He had very little previous experience in decision making. He certainly was inexperienced in money matters. He had been allowed to spend his allowance in any manner he desired when he was at home so that this carried over into college life. He became a

free spender and soon was B.M.O.C. — Big Man On
Campus. He was the life of the party — at least the
lifeline, as his checking account was fairly fluid. All
he needed was a "Dear Mom" letter and the supply
was replenished.

Other problems developed. The partying began
on weekends, but then he started missing Monday
classes. As he became more and more involved socially, he either was too tired to get up, or had a hang-
over and didn't feel like getting up. He also started
missing classes during the week. He was given plenty
of warning but was unprepared to face reality—failure—failure to realize he no longer had parents
near enough to buffer his falls.

As I sat listening to the other parents discussing
our current problem, I was comparing Roger at five and
Jerry at 18—the beginning of school and the end.

I spent a great deal of time with Roger's mother.
He didn't change overnight, but as a result of our
discussions, his mother became less anxious which, in
turn, took off some of the pressure. She began by
talking with Roger and letting him know what she
expected in the way of behavior and what the consequences would be if he disobeyed. She then began
to see the need for consistency in dealing with him.
As she became more relaxed, she could trust him to
play out of her sight.

He started coming to her to discuss problems with
the boy next door, and before long she was able to
let him work out the solutions for himself. She not
only developed trust in him, but he also developed trust
in her. This was a beginning step toward his establishment of independence.

This kind of problem might have been averted,
or even avoided, much earlier in Roger's development.
A child begins the emancipation process early in life—
if his parents feel secure and plan ways for it to happen.

One mother I know starts very early giving responsibilities to her children. As soon as they can walk,

she expects them to help with picking up their toys. She not only expects them to do the chores, but she also takes the time to see that the jobs are done. She agrees that this is time consuming, but it pays dividends later. As the children mature, she finds ways of helping them develop. They learn to dress themselves very early, they assist with the care of the younger children, and learn to accept their share of the work load. She, in turn, gives them the praise, love, and feeling of well-being that all children need as they strive toward a well-adjusted adulthood.

As the older children reach maturity, and are ready for decision making on a major scale, they will have developed confidence in and respect for their parents so that the apron strings will be easily untied. This is a two-way street. Crisis situations arise infrequently in this home, but those which do arise are solved with logic rather than tears.

Many parents are in the habit of making all the decisions at home so that they are blind to what is really going on when one of their children rebels.

How often I have heard young teenage girls say, "My mother doesn't understand me." I usually have to agree with them. Although young people often twist the facts to fit their conception of the problems, it usually turns out that the solution might have been easier if the parents had listened earlier and planned ahead. It can't be stressed too often that we must listen to children and pay attention to their actions as well as their words. They often tell us more by what they do than by what they say.

Just as a child learns to walk, parents must also learn to take first steps. One of the first is a perception or awareness of a need for close family relationships—a sharing relationship, not a telling one. Get involved with children in the family.

Another step parents must take is that of understanding the child from his viewpoint. How does he feel about rules and regulations? Are they consistent with his expectations, or are they impossible for him to achieve? The child who can't reach the goals set by his parents is often the one who gives up and becomes forever dependent, or strikes out and becomes delinquent.

A third step parents must take to lessen the strain of emancipation is to help their children feel loved. It is not enough to say, "I love you," but one must feel that love and know that it is real.

Finally, parents must have faith in themselves while they believe in and trust their children: have faith that they are capable of directing their children toward the good life; believe that their teachings will reach their children and help them make the right decisions; then, trust them to carry out these decisions.

What does all this say? Merely that independence will be gained in one way or another. It need not be difficult. The easiest way to avoid trauma is to begin early in a child's life to let him make some decisions. He won't always make the right ones, but if he is allowed to make some mistakes early in life, and is supported by his parents, he will have developed a technique for communicating.

Begin decision making early by allowing children to select the clothes they would like to wear for the day, or let them decide whether to go to bed at a pre-set time or 30 minutes later. Their decisions will not always please their mother, but she will be in a position to discuss her viewpoint with the child, at the same time listening to his ideas.

I know a mother who takes her four-year-old shopping and lets her buy her own clothes—with guidance, of course. As the child matures, she will have had a great deal of experience in not only handling money, but also in knowing how to budget wisely. When she is ready to manage her own affairs, the handling of money will be routine.

Another excellent place to take children for decision making is the library. Long before a child reads words, he reads pictures. Let him select the books he likes. Too often adults make the selections and kill the enthusiasm which is generated by a vivid imagination as the child reads things in pictures which no one else can see. A book selected by someone else may return to the library unopened.

There are more decisions to be made when the five-year-old enters school. Let him decide whether or not he will eat lunch in the cafeteria, take a sack lunch, or go home to eat. This seems like a very minor thing, and it is, but it is another step toward independence, and he will be ever so happy with a choice instead of, "You must . . . ."

Are allowances necessary evils? You bet, if the family can afford one and the children are mature enough to understand our monetary system. Too often this is just money without controls, as was the case with Jerry. Unless a child learns some kind of management from having money, he may just as well ask his parents each time he wants to buy something. He needs help in making decisions about saving his money, but he also needs experience in making decisions about how it should be spent. He learns early that when his money is gone, his purchasing power vanishes.

Pre-teens and teens will have more pressures imposed from peers and others outside the family. There will be decisions to make regarding friendships, dates, and hours to be home from the various activities. This can become a time of stress and strain if no planning has been done previously.

At what age do girls wear nylons and lipstick? When are boys ready to visit the bowling alleys alone? These questions must be answered by the individual family. If the children are allowed to discuss these things with their parents, the decisions are more likely to be understood and accepted by both parties.

If the lines of communication are kept open there will be plenty of activity and a closeness which is gratifying. On the other hand, if the lines are closed, the children will probably be waiting for a chance to escape via early marriage, Army service, or simply going away to school. There is a choice for parents. Make the right one!

by Charles Fraser, MD

# 15. Childhood Fears

FEAR is an emotion marked by dread, apprehension or alarm. It is a powerful emotion, ranking with sex and hunger. It is also a learned emotion. Some fears are instinctive—that is, you are born with them—such as fear of falling and fear of unexpected loud noises. But most fears are learned. Learned from whom? Mostly parents.

Mrs. Elaine Turney, mother of four, is afraid of lightning, mice, snakes, moth millers, and nighttime intruders. Mrs. Turney's children are afraid to sleep in a dark room, often they won't let her out of their sight, and they routinely awaken screaming in the middle of the night. Surely this is coincidence. Or is it?

As a practicing pediatrician, I find this problem of children's fears to be a very common one. It causes anguish, not only to the fearful child, but to the parent who doesn't know how to handle such fears. Let's examine first some causes.

Parents don't try to teach fear to their children, but there are a thousand subtle ways to convey when one is afraid without saying a word.

Primarily it is an unconscious transference of feeling by small gestures, facial expressions, and acts of avoidance that convey to the child the sensation that this is a situation to be alarmed about. The parent who is forever checking all the locks on doors and windows throughout the house is doing little to instill confidence in the security of the home. The mother who is always screaming, "Get down from there! You'll fall!" is not helping her child develop the skills and abilities that he needs to handle himself in later situations. What boy is ever going to become a good quarterback if his mother is always yelling, "Look out for the windows with that football!"

Parents play a more important role than they suspect in the establishment of attitudes of fear or courage in their children. It has been demonstrated that a child is far more likely to acquire from his parents the fears that they, unconsciously or not, show that they have. Some of these are: fear of the dark, fear of thunder and lightning, fear of animals, and fear of people in authority. Also, it is harder to rid a child of a fear likewise possessed by his parents than one picked up in some other way. The parents' upbringing and experiences have brought about habits of response that are so much a part of them that they have no idea how often they show their feelings. The parents truly interested in bringing up children free of fear will make an honest effort to conquer their own fears, presuming, of course, that they are aware of them.

On occasion, fears are the result of misinterpretation by the child of an innocent act by the parent. A mother may close the window when it rains to keep the carpet from getting wet. The onlooking child may interpret this as being afraid of thunder and lightning. The parent may say innocently, "Let's scoot home, it's getting dark," meaning it's bedtime, but the child might interpret it as a fear of the night. Since the child is often reluctant to mention that he is afraid, he will keep it to himself. But the fear may come out later in a much different situation, such as a dream, so that it is not at all clear where he got the original fear.

The fear of failure or a markedly timid child may be the result of extremely harsh parental criticism. If he is domineered and blustered at for every minor deviance from the straight and narrow, he may come to expect this treatment on all sides and develop a

sense of discouragement and failure, resulting in un-
willingness and hesitation in tackling anything new or
difficult. It is questionable whether a child who has
been made timid and shrinking by harsh, stern treatment can ever again regain a natural, open manner
and successfully assert himself. How can the child
who has been yelled at for getting his hands dirty
while building sand castles ever develop the freedom
of thought necessary to be an architect?

Fears of the unknown are common. Fears of death,
handicaps or disfigurement, uncontrollable elements
(such as thunder and lightning), getting old, unusual
differences of himself in comparison to others (such as
skin color), all may stimulate fears that are not easily
voiced. They may lie dormant for long periods and
suddenly break out. An example would be the child
who awakened screaming at night because he had had
a nightmare involving his house being blown away by
the wind. This dated back to having seen a TV news-
cast of a hurricane blowing over houses several weeks
previously.

How can we prevent such fears or remove them
once they have become established?

The infant should be protected from violent activity,
sudden noises, in short—the unexpected. This is not
to say that he should be shielded from the world, but
at that point where interest begins to turn to fright, the
stimulus should be removed or lessened. As the child
grows, help him to understand the world about him.
Take advantage of his curiosity to further his knowledge. Encourage communication. Be a ready refer-
ence source so that there will be no hesitation in
asking about the new or unknown. The more he knows
about something, the less likely he will be to fear it.

One of the quickest ways to rid a child of a fear
is to connect the feared object or situation with a
strongly pleasant feeling. Thus, if a child has become
afraid of the dark, play a game involving searching
dark places for rewards such as candy or wearing a

blindfold in play. In the case of fear of animals, the child who has developed a fear of dogs might be exposed to the delightful antics of a puppy who is so obviously harmless that the child will lose the unhappy association with other dogs. The fear of night might be alleviated by searching for a certain constellation of stars; the fear of lightning eased by sitting and watching for different outlines against the black sky.

This is simply taking advantage of his curiosity, but it has to be done by a parent who has no fear of the same situation. Removing the cause of fear does not really help, for the fear lingers on. Pleasant re-associations are far more effective, such as listening at the darkened bedroom window for the songs of night birds or crickets, rather than leaning heavily on night lights and reassurance.

Children are often relieved of fears when they begin to participate more in group play. They find that their fear is not justified when something frightening to them, such as an animal, may actually be enjoyed by the group. Sometimes, however, if other children seem unafraid the child may actually hide his fear rather than be the object of teasing. If a child seems to enjoy a marked preference for solitude, it should be gently explored in a sympathetic manner to make sure that it is not fear, but a liking for being alone that makes him a "loner."

When it is known that a new situation is going to be encountered, a bit of preparation in the way of explanation of what the child is about to see or do will take away the surprise and fear. Sometimes surprise is desirable, but fear seldom is.

A child needs concrete help in overcoming fear in the form of pleasant associations, actual experiences, and demonstrations. He wants no part of coercion, ignoring, or explanations and reassurances that have nothing to back them up. A few minutes playing with a puppy will do more than hours of reassurance about dogs.

In the private practice of pediatrics I see many Mrs. Turneys and an endless list of fears. Some mothers seem a bit ruffled when I begin to ask their methods of managing different situations rather than giving them a five-minute "quick cure" for a child with a specific fear. But seldom does one fear occur alone, and although it takes a lot longer in uncovering the origins of a fear, one can do a lot better job if the management and discipline and communication background of the family is known.

Mrs. Turney did conquer her own fears. Her apprehensions eased and she worked with the little ones along some of the general lines suggested here. They quit clinging to her, became interested in new and different things, and rarely experience a broken night's sleep.

One last note. Honesty must prevail in all aspects of helping children to overcome abnormal fears. (This applies to other areas as well, but its importance here can't be overemphasized.) Consider the child who is told by his mother he is about to get an injection, "It's not going to hurt." Do you think he'll believe her later that evening when she tells him there are no monsters lurking in his darkened bedroom?

by Lois Griffith

# 16. Children And Money

SUMMER before last, I found myself involved in a bookkeeping entanglement that would have taken a C.P.A. to resolve. Our nine-year-old son, David, longed for a rock hammer. He came to me with the problem.

"Mom," he snitched bits of cookie dough as he talked, "I've just got to get that rock hammer. I've saved up three dollars, but the hammer costs seven dollars. Could you advance my allowance for eight weeks so I could get it now?"

"I think it would be best," I replied, "if you'd wait until you've saved the amount of money you need."

"But, Mom," he groaned, "it's the first of August now. If I have to wait eight weeks, school will be on, and I won't get a chance to use the hammer at all. Besides, we're going to the mountains next weekend, and just think what I could do with it there."

His argument seemed reasonable, but I decided to unshoulder part of the weighty decision on my husband. "We'll see what Dad says," I told David.

David's reasoning, plus the pleading look in his big brown eyes, won over his dad. We advanced the allowance, David purchased the hammer, and monetary peace reigned the household—for two weeks.

With David still three dollars in the red, he and his older brother, Dan, plunged into the building of a go-cart. "We need nails," David explained.

"Dan has some money, hasn't he?" I questioned.

"Yeah, but since we're building the cart together, I have to pay half. Can't you advance me a little more money?"

I capitulated. The boys were having such a good time pounding and sawing. Besides, I reasoned, building a go-cart was an excellent learning process, and furthermore, it kept them out of my cookie dough.

Two days later, they needed more cash for "some wheels the kid down the block will sell us real cheap."

One day passed, and "got to go to the hardware store and get a piece of good strong rope."

A day later, "We've run out of paint, Mom. Do those cans of spray paint cost very much?"

I gave in all down the line. Adding several figures here, subtracting one there as allowance day rolled around, I suddenly found myself keeping two sets of books. Diane, our seven-year-old, decided she would open a school for the neighborhood preschoolers. This required paper, colors, and scissors. Again I advanced the needed cash.

One week before school started I found the rock hammer rusting on the damp lawn. The go-cart crouched in the rear of the garage all but ruined by misuse and neglect. Diane's student body had fled to the more delightful pleasures of vacant lot freedom, and the only trace of the school supplies were the bits of crayons that ground beneath my feet.

I hit the roof, telling the children exactly what I thought of their misuse and neglect. Later, reflecting on the whole situation, I sadly admitted at least part of the fault was mine. By handing out the money to them, whether it was due or not, I'd unconsciously inferred that money had no real value, and as a correlation, that the things they purchased with the money had no value.

Never again, I vowed. My eyes were now open to another of the seemingly endless problems of raising children. I later observed some of my friends and neighbors coping with the same challenge.

One neighbor handled the problem firmly, but temperately. The children received a fixed allowance, substantial enough, she thought, to purchase all they normally needed. If they desired something extra special, they came to her for extraordinary jobs for which they pocketed additional money. Cleaning the attic, washing all the windows in the house, scrubbing and waxing a floor, cleaning the garage, all ranked as "above and beyond" chores, but the pay was never exorbitant.

Her children seldom misused anything, and certainly knew the work involved in obtaining money. As a side benefit, I never saw them casually spilling food on a floor or rubbing their hands across a windowpane.

At the opposite end of the teeter-totter sat a friend of mine whose child wrecked almost everything he touched. Her home was a shambles of broken toys and mangled furniture. Not only did he value nothing of his own or of his parents, but he also felt no compunction about destroying others' possessions. During the course of their visits, he smashed my children's toys, cut grooves in the walls of two rooms, and shattered a large mirror. The day he deeply scratched my old but still cherished piano by using its top as a model airplane landing field remains fixed forever in my mind. Instead of chastising the child, the mother handed him a five-dollar bill and told him to "go on down to the shopping center and get out of my hair."

What, I wondered, would happen to that boy as he grew up? What happened to any of the children who received no training as to the value of money and the value of the things money purchased? Was the boy who used the piano as a landing strip an example so extreme that he did not figure into the picture?

"I'm afraid I've seen worse cases," psychologist friend Bob answered my question. "Oh, sure, destroying almost everything he touches is pretty bad," and he laughed at my incredulous expression. "But, I've seen children who have literally wrecked a house."

My memory did a time slip, and I recalled one home we'd inspected as we'd house-hunted a few years ago.

The house perched in a delightful spot—a view, lots of trees, and quite removed from heavily traveled streets. The house was beautifully designed, and only two years old, but alas, was no longer beautiful.

Gouged floors, marred walls, stained carpets greeted us as we surveyed the house. The stone fireplace stood pocked with missing rocks. Plumbing fixtures drooped away from walls, light fixtures dangled precariously loose from ceilings. "What happened?" I gasped to the real estate agent. "Did vandals break in?"

"No," he replied. "The children. The former owner's children did this."

I hardly believed him, but promptly forgot about the house and the possibly destructive children. The house needed thousands of dollars of repairs before it was habitable. We had neither the money nor the time.

"Admittedly," Bob interrupted by recollections, "there are probably other factors involved with such totally destructive children. But I feel that the casual distribution of money by parents has a great deal to do with it. If money is so available, the kids reason, then it isn't hard to get. If it isn't hard to get, then it doesn't have much value. If money is devalued, then what it can buy is devalued."

"Just as David with his rock hammer," I voiced. "It was too easy to get. It didn't mean enough to him."

Bob nodded. "But that happened over a year ago. Have things changed at your house?"

"Yes, they have," I answered, and went on to describe the results of not advancing allowances. Dan, our oldest, had never presented a problem in regard to money or respect for things. He'd apparently been born with a sense of monetary value. David seldom destroyed anything, but often neglected his belongings. At the start of the "no money until it's due" program, David blew every cent of his weekly dole. A few months later, his hands itching for new handlebars for his bike, he managed to slowly save enough to make the purchase. By the time our summer vacation rolled around, he'd collected a remarkable-for-him four dollars, and bought a rock collection he'd seen and longed for the summer before.

He batted not an eye when his older brother and younger sister purchased souvenirs at other stopping-off spots. "I got what I wanted," he explained, and, once home, carefully lined a cardboard box with scrap-bag materials, and meticulously labeled each rock.

Little Diane still disposes of every penny every week. "Is their learning a matter of time, a matter of growing up?" I asked Bob.

"Partially," Bob replied. "Some children seem born with a monetary value, but, with most of them, it's a matter of learning." Bob squinted out the window, and indicated a wrecked car being towed up the street. "It's a lesson all children need to learn," and went on to explain why.

This lack of monetary values in childhood, if not corrected, often extends into adolescence and adulthood. Johnny wrecks his dad's car, and feels little, if any, regret. Mary ruins an expensive dress, and nonchalantly stuffs it into the back of the closet. Billy borrows from his dad's tie rack, and "forgets" to return the tie. Susan uses her mother's perfume, and "accidentally" spills it on the dresser top. And, when Johnny, Mary, Billy and Susan become adults, they fail to care for home, automobile, clothes, or property.

"Don't they ever learn, even as adults?" I asked Bob.

"Some do," he admitted. "They run out of money for repairs, for new clothes, and finally learn—the hard way. Some never learn. They spend their whole lives in a financial hole. Not because they're poor earners, but poor learners. And speaking of learning," Bob went on, "there is another lesson children must learn besides the value of money and what it can buy. And this lesson, too, often goes hand in glove with proper money management. They must learn to wait."

"Learn to wait?" I echoed.

"Yes," Bob replied. "David denied himself the weekly candy bars, bottles of soda pop, toys of small value. He waited. He waited until he'd saved enough to buy the rock collection. Consequently, he values the rocks, but, just as important, he learned to wait for something he felt was valuable."

Bob went on to give examples of children not learning to wait. Linda and Tom can't wait to get married. They've always gotten what they wanted, immediately, and now they want each other. They marry right after high school, and Tom works at a poor paying job. Nothing but a poor paying job is open to Tom. He took college preparatory classes in high school, but didn't go on to college. If he'd taken vocational courses, or gone on to a trade school or apprenticeship, many more doors would be open, but he didn't.

Tom soon learns that man may not live on bread alone, but neither does he live on love alone. Romance pales before harsh reality, but Tom is trapped by the lack of education. Trapped because he didn't learn to wait.

Rex and Cathy, back from their honeymoon, rush out to buy a new home. Although the monthly payments already severely deplete Rex's salary, the couple can't wait to luxuriate in fashionable surroundings. They buy a houseful of furniture, all on the "convenient monthly payment plan." Rex and Cathy finally wake up to find themselves trapped by financial insolvency. Trapped because they hadn't learned to wait.

Adolescents, lured by the imagined pleasures of liquor, drugs, or sex, find themselves trapped by alcoholism, drug addiction, or pregnancy. Instead of being willing to wait for the more valued judgment of maturity, they "blow" their minds on LSD, "hook" themselves on heroin, "brand" themselves with promiscuity.

Last week, Diane found herself at the receiving

end of a lecture. I'd discovered the greater share of her birthday presents in a jumbled heap on her bedroom floor. "The people who gave you these gifts," I informed Diane, "spent hard-earned money for them. And what's more, they spent a good deal of time and effort in picking out something they knew you would like. I want you to play with your toys, but you must take care of them."

Dan walked in at this point, regarded me with a glint in his eyes, and said, "Don't blow your cool, Mom. She hasn't learned yet."

I kept right on lecturing. Far better to blow my cool now than lose it later if my daughter found herself in a mess because I failed to teach her respect for money and what it can buy, or neglected to teach her the wisdom of waiting.

by Charles Fraser, MD

# 17. Is Your Child
# a Potential Drug User?

MY credentials are less than impeccable, but they have validity. I am a concerned parent of four children, one in high school, one in junior high school, and two in grade school. In addition I have had more than ten years' experience in the private practice of pediatrics in a metropolitan suburb encompassing all levels of culture and affluence. Almost daily some situation touches my life that exemplifies three of the precipitating factors of drug usage in today's society: drug-orientation, identity, and lack of communication.

Let me share some examples with you. One of my phone calls last week was from a mother who wanted to know what to do about her six-year-old daughter wetting the bed. We discussed the situation a bit and agreed on some suggestions as to positive approaches. I thought we were making progress until she asked, "Doc, this has me so upset, I wonder if you could give me a prescription for some tranquilizers?" Now I couldn't stay in business very long if I had answered what I really felt, but we were able to work out her feelings with a tiny bit of insight into the consideration that she could scarcely expect her daughter to cope with anything later if her mother resorted to nipping on "instant happiness pills" every time a minor problem raised its ugly head. In short, another symptom of our drug-oriented society.

Recently, I went pheasant hunting in one of our rural areas. I stayed overnight at a ranch house where there were two teenage boys. I asked them if anyone was using "grass" in their high school. "Heck no, we don't have time for stuff like that. Dad needs us too badly and, besides, we're spending an awful lot of time trying to get our herd of Herefords in shape so we can cop one of the county prizes." He went on to add that there were rumors that some of the "town boys" may have given "pot" a whirl, but that it was only a rumor.

They knew the vernacular, but here were two young men with a purpose. There was neither a place for drugs in their life, nor a need for them.

And this one hurts, for I saw it coming. A teenage girl whom I have known for some years awakened her mother in the early hours of the morning with stomach cramps that could only have been related to the recent flu epidemic in our area. Four hours later she delivered a beautiful, pink, squalling, healthy, full-term baby in the local hospital. After the smoke had cleared a little and the parents had been scraped off the ceiling, I asked her why she had not confided in them. "I was afraid to tell them." One might safely say that there was a communication problem in this family.

These are personal episodes that happened to someone else, but they might touch anyone, even tonight—if we don't become aware of what is happening in our home and community—now.

To begin, why do kids take drugs? Research reveals five basic reasons:

1. To prove courage by risk-taking.

2. To act out rebellion and hostility to authority.

3. To facilitate sexual desire and responsiveness.

4. To relieve loneliness and to provide a new experience.

5. To attempt to find a meaning of life.

It is important to recognize that there is no such thing as a stereotyped user, the person who relies on repeated drug utilization. The person who uses drugs is not necessarily alienated or in rebellion or emotionally disturbed. Each case has to be judged individually.

But once the use of drugs has begun, the users soon belong to one of three major classes:

1. The experience seekers.

2. The oblivion seekers.

3. The personality-change seekers.

The experience seeker is an individual who, either because of social pressures or because of fascination with the dangers of arrest, addiction, or dying, takes a limited number of forays into the world of drugs. Unless he is unfortunate enough to have a bad "trip," the outlook for this person is good. He needs a concerned listener who knows drugs and their dangers, who is honest—for there is no greater crime to a teenager than hypocrisy; a person who can relate to him in a manner that will help him outline his goals and to find himself as an individual. The experience seeker usually tries to shock his parents so that they become more concerned. He may be successful by having his parents invest more of themselves in his behalf.

The oblivion seeker finds the drugged state a pleasant respite from the stresses of the world. It reminds me of the recent cartoon depicting the bearded fellow on the psychiatrist's couch saying, "My dreams are groovy, man. It's being awake that bugs me." This fellow may blame the war, the world, society, and others, but is really burdened by feelings of incompetence and inadequacy with respect to his efforts in trying to cope with the war, the world, and society. He has a poor self-image and holds himself in low esteem.

The typical product of our times has plenty of plaudits for winners, but very little for the honest pluggers.

This is why many authorities are overjoyed to see

the trend toward the ungraded educational system where an individual is placed in competition to be a winner with himself—not as a failure when compared to others.

The adolescent has to sit back and take an honest inventory of his strengths and weaknesses—not what his dad and mom think he should be. He should be encouraged to develop fully along lines that are palatable to him—not act out his parents' vicarious desires that he should be what they always wanted to be, but never were. This fellow is easy to identify. He comes home with one or two rubber stamps all over his report card: "Not working up to capacity," or, "Could do better if he would only apply himself."

The third category, the personality-change seeker, feels compelled to combine drugs and to increase dosages as his disappointments and his frustrations mount. He has an underlying basic personality problem, such as a character disorder. These individuals were troubled before they discovered drugs and drugs have only added to their difficulties.

But is my child on drugs? Has he tried them? How can I know?

Is he on drugs? Probably not. Has he tried them? Possibly. How will I know it? This is a more difficult question, but may be answered by availing yourself of literature that is readily available from your schools, interested community groups, or your physician. A little homework will make you familiar with the names of drugs, their actions, their symptoms, and will enable you to begin talking with your kids.

When you do start talking to your teenagers, remember there are some basic rules:

Be honest.

No sensationalism and scare techniques.

If you don't know the answer—say so.

Don't moralize.

Confidential communication must be respected. Here's where you will have better luck than the physician who has to respect his patient's privacy, and knows the problem, but has to hint, imply, and allude to the parents in an attempt to work toward insight.

Remember also:

Your teenager probably knows more about drugs than you do.

He or she probably has no insight into the emotional and social dangers involved.

However, he is aware of the dangers in a physical sense.

This all smacks of preaching, moralizing, and sermonizing. And, in fact, *are* we placing too much emphasis on drugs? Will the kids go out and try them just because we've been asking so many questions around home that "Mom and Dad must expect me to." Not if we can keep observations candid, casual, and honest.

Would there be too much emphasis if we began talking at the junior high level? I don't think so. If communication is slipping, it may not yet be completely gone—there's still time.

All your discussions must show the desire to learn and not to label too quickly. Like the college kid who was afraid to come home for Christmas vacation because he wasn't like a "typical" college kid. So he grew a beard, smoked a "stick," and sneaked out one night to see a controversial play. Such is the danger of stereotyping. But stereotype or not, if you think we aren't being affected by the kids, take a quick glance around at your next party and see how the sideburns have been coming down.

A physician's medical training makes him want to be able to tie such a problem up into some sort of package so that he can look at it from all sides. To me, the most satisfactory approach so far has been to classify this primarily as a problem of identity.

Identity is defined as what a person thinks about himself and what he thinks other people think about him and his feelings about these. In short—who am I?

We see people throughout society, at all levels, searching for identity. From business executives managing corporations to the poverty-stricken individual lost in the ghetto; people are trying to find out who they are. The reasons are many. Sheer numbers of people, mobility, breakup of old traditions, loss of identity symbols, lack of the sense of community, and a trend toward scientific thinking that leads us to question ceremony and ritual which used to be meaningful.

Such is the essence of the "why" of drug taking. But think of the problem as if you were a kid today. You're smart, but there are smarter guys. You catch a pretty good pass, but can't quite make the team. You can talk well, but not with enough authority to make anyone listen. You can get work, but nothing of interest because of lack of "experience." There's nothing at home that you really have to do, except a little work, and your parents could get along without you with ease. You had an opinion once, but were promptly shot down without regard for your feelings.

With this environment, how would you try to establish yourself as a person—as an individual?

Pretty grim, isn't it? How's a guy to cope with all these problems? There are several ways one can get the feeling of being someone, to escape from all of this, at least for a few hours. Why not? Mom and Dad nip on "pick-me-ups" and "lay-me-downs" as well as "be-gentle-on-my-minds" all the time. So pass the word to one of your buddies, not to "some dirty old man," as is commonly believed, and soon there'll be a "stick" or "cap" or "acid" making an appearance.

At a time in his life when a teenager needs to implant complicated mathematical formulae in his mind, drugs scramble his brain. When he is beginning to experience the exhilaration and responsibilities of love and sexuality, drugs tend to make such experiences complicated, artificial, and impermanent. At a time when adolescents must deal with the healthy issues of independence, career decisions and the meaning of life, drugs offer a seductive way of ducking the issues, hiding out, and giving up. It's known as the "chemical cop-out."

In almost every publication one peruses, there is at least one article commenting in a critical way upon the teenager, drugs, society, and the home. Let's take a few moments to list the positive actions available to help us meet this problem. What weapons can we muster to combat this tide of concern?

1. Remember that the individual must find what meets his own unique needs and that which fits someone else's concept of him.

2. Young people must have responsible family and community roles.

3. They must find honesty in the home, in the school, and in the community.

4. They may find their interest in group activities—in sports (unpressured) or in club activities (clubs with a purpose).

5. They may express themselves as individuals in art, drama, music and crafts.

6. They may express themselves in concern for others. It might be politics, human relations, direct service to others, or working with younger children.

7. They'll have a better chance in a school geared to the individual, a school without failure.

8. Learn family communication. Set up workshops, if needed, to teach this lost art.

9. Have your home available for entertaining your children and their friends.

10. Ask the kids what their outstanding recreational needs are. Do not ask them to fit into your concept of these needs.

11. Learn to listen.

12. Keep in touch with your children. Know what they are saying, seeing, hearing, and doing. You don't have to enjoy the same things—just don't turn them off.

13. Parent-student discussion groups would be a productive way to improve communication. There's something about the moral support of a group with similar problems that encourages give and take.

14. Replace graded regurgitation with an educational process relevant to the world.

In other words, there is a better way to "turn on."

by Anonymous

# 18. My Years On Drugs

I'M one of the thousands of young people who turned to drugs to try to solve the problems of growing up. I hope I can help parents to understand their kids who move toward drugs; and maybe help others understand those parents whose kids are on the stuff.

I guess everybody knows—or thinks he knows—drug usage is becoming a more and more common way of running away from the problems we must face. But it's always somebody else's kid who's going to be foolish enough to get involved in the drug culture: somebody very poor or some kid who's got everything. But the simple fact is that drugs are available in almost any community in the nation.

I come from a rather average family—average income, anyway. There are ten kids in my family. My dad died when I was twelve. I was luckier than a lot of kids who got on drugs because I didn't start until I was out of high school. So I was well into adolescence before I began to try to escape from the pressures of growing up. In that way I'm different from a lot of kids today. The sharpest increase in drug usage is among high school and even pre-high school kids.

I went with a friend to New York City when I was eighteen. We were with a group of kids who started smoking marijuana. I was nervous, but I didn't want to refuse. And I really wanted to try it. The fact that I went to New York to begin using drugs isn't really important; I knew they were available in my own community.

When I began on marijuana, I did so with the firm resolve that I would never go any farther. But I soon found myself using a wide variety of drugs.

My first experiences were very beautiful. The grass gave me a certain peace, and put me at ease. It helped me to feel comfortable and forget the tensions of the day. My tensions were mainly from loneliness. I was separated from my family; and as much as I may have wanted to be away from my family, it was hard finding new friends and trying to establish myself. I didn't know really who I was or what I wanted to do with my life. And somehow that nags you, even though you rarely look at the question squarely.

For some reason, I often got the feeling that grown-ups didn't really appreciate the tensions that younger people feel, although teen-age tensions so closely resemble those of the adult. Adults seemed to recognize the desirability of a cocktail party or a couple of drinks after a day's work and it looked to me as if adults do with martinis and manhattans pretty much the same thing we did with marijuana.

Physically, marijuana is less harmful than alcohol and its effects, for the most part, are more desirable. Grass gives a free, floating feeling like alcohol, but without a sluggishness and heavy feeling. Marijuana also increases the awareness of your surroundings and the inner experiences you are having. I'm not recommending marijuana as a substitute for alcohol, but these are the reasons I smoked grass. If you happen to find great enjoyment in a drink and it helps you to feel more comfortable in a social gathering, you can understand more easily what prompts a kid to smoke grass.

I did find one real danger in grass. It placed me out of the environment I was used to. I started smoking marijuana, and sought out other kids who were on it. I began to isolate myself from friends who would have helped me to see that what I was doing was wrong.

I can't plot a course that I followed in using drugs.

Everything just seemed to follow until I had a hard time turning back. I found that drugs could give me a release from the problems and tensions I faced every day. They also gave me a group to identify with; and along with that came the long hair and weird clothes—everything that could show I was in rebellion against society. I moved back to my home town and, without realizing it, I became dependent on drugs for my escape from the tensions and difficulties I had to face. I found it so easy to blame society for all that depressed me; and I could get away from society while on drugs. From this dependence on drugs (marijuana), and from association with the others who were using them, I began slipping into things like speed and LSD.

Speed gave me a sense of power. When I was on speed I felt I was king of the world, and I had great energy. I'm really quite short and scrawny, but speed compensated for the inferiority I felt. It also helped me face the loneliness I was experiencing from being away from my family and childhood ties. Using speed put me with a group of kids who could fill this void in my life and who would encourage me in my complaints against society and family life. I wanted to be accepted. I wanted to live a life that was compatible with my ideals; so I lived a hippie-type life, relying on drugs more and more. It took a year of living this way—a year of seeing what drugs were doing to me and my friends—to bring me to my senses.

I never took drugs to the extent that I harmed myself physically. I did use them enough to experience both their good and bad effects, and to suffer emotionally from the depression and guilt they caused. At first, speed and pep pills were great to be on. My mind was sharp and my body was ready for action and on the move. I just felt good all over. With heavier doses I began to experience shaking and my body became tense. And with these came the confusion and withdrawal of a speed freak. In smaller doses, the drug helped me to communicate with others; but the increased dosage put me into such a confused state that nothing came through clearly. Just trying to get an idea out in the form of a sentence became almost impossible. The drug also made me suspicious of anyone or anything around me; any quick movement caused fear.

After I used speed I would find myself in a state of depression, deeper than any I've ever experienced. I would hate to count the hours I spent lying on my bed just staring at the ceiling. These were the worst times of that year. Any disturbance would irritate me. If Mom came into my room and asked me to do something, the only answer she got was, "O God, will you leave me alone." In fact, if anyone so much as bid me the time of day it made me angry.

I spent most of my time in my room. I dreamed great dreams of what I could be; or else I thought of suicide. Suicide seemed to be the only answer to the guilt and worry I had developed over using drugs. I remember one occasion when I was very confused and disorganized. I spent most of my time getting stoned but as I came down I got worried and depressed, so I went out and got stoned again. Then I slowly began to realize that this stuff was bad for me, but turning around seemed impossible. All my friends used the stuff and when I was down, the depression was so great that the only answer was to get stoned again.

I think the most beautiful and the most dangerous drug I used was acid. You probably know it as LSD. I really don't know how to describe it. Most of all, it opened a beautiful and totally new world to me.

The hallucinations were beautiful. Walls moved; patterns blended into new patterns; and all combined into a world of color, movement and sound. Any insignificant object could become of great interest. I remember spending a couple of hours with an orange. Each little part held special interest as it moved and

seemed to draw me into it, experiencing its color, taste
and feeling. Every object in the room had its own
texture. As these textures moved, they captured my
attention, drew me further into them; experiencing
them as color, movement and feeling.

On an LSD trip, everything I caught sight of seemed
to have its own flashing light. Each object captured
my attention and as I would turn to drink it in, some
other object flashed its light. I would turn to that object, only to catch sight of another out of the corner
of my eye. I continued this way, until I was almost
completely disorientated. At the same time there is a
tremendous contradiction in feelings. Everything is
experienced in two ways. I would raise my arms, and
feel like I was floating; but at the same time my arms
felt so heavy I could hardly lift them. I would feel hot
and sweaty; at the same time I was shivering with
cold. I could see myself—particularly my stupidity
for being on drugs—and it would make me laugh; but
it also made me cry because the truth of the situation
was so sad.

The drug was beautiful. But it was some really
bad experiences on it that made me eventually seek
help and get off the stuff.

Two particularly bad experiences I remember well.

The first time I ever used acid I ended up in a little
white room all by myself. I was in a friend's apart-
ment. I suddenly found I couldn't stop the hallucinations. Everything started moving faster; I got
scared. I had to talk to someone. I called Suicide Control—a number you can call any time of day or night.
I talked to the lady for about three hours. She eventually talked me down. I remember feeling really rotten
after this. How had I gotten so far from what I wanted
to be?

The other really bad experience I had on acid was
much worse. A really good friend used drugs much
heavier than I did. I remember admiring her; she was
an artist and one of the most talented young people

I had ever met. But by now any creativity had completely stopped. She and I usually dropped acid together. There were two other kids with us that night who had never used drugs before. They wanted to take some speed. I tried to talk them out of it, but how could I convince someone not to do something they had heard me brag about?

Everything was really beautiful. In fact, I was even farther out than I had ever gone before. One of the kids said something to Sue that scared her. She began to freak! She was out of control; we couldn't reach her. She began to shake violently and all I could see of her was a moving blur. The two kids got really scared and started to cry. They started asking me, "What's wrong? What's happening to Sue?" All I wanted at that moment was to be so stoned that I'd never come down again. But I began to crash. I no longer saw the beauty of the drug; all I saw was two kids scared and crying to me for help and a good friend stoned out of my reach. Sue managed to say, "Get them out of here!" She knew how to handle herself on acid so we left the room. We went to my house and sat there till morning.

Crashing is coming down real fast. I just sat shaking in a corner of my living room. The two kids sat silently next to each other. They were too afraid to say anything, but they kept staring at me. Then, I realized how I must have looked. They had looked up to me, and I had led them into this. There I was, shaking like a scared little kid.

At 8 o'clock the next morning the two kids and I went to school. We sat in the cafeteria for two hours worrying about Sue. She showed up about 10; she hadn't come down yet. She was still hallucinating. The hallucinations weren't beautiful; they almost seemed to be chasing her. We spent about two hours in silence. She just hung on to my hand; her hand shook like she was scared. She was so stoned that she couldn't get a sentence out straight. She stuttered

over every word she tried to say. I just sat there
blaming myself for the whole thing. I started two kids
on drugs; I had supported Sue until she went so far
out that maybe she'd never come back. I felt I had
betrayed myself and my friends. At that moment I
hated myself. I decided to get help.

I don't know why stopping was so much easier for
me than it is for a lot of kids. I think most kids reach
this point on drugs. There are two courses to take—
back out, or go for heavier doses. I think my return
was easier because of my mother. She had to know
something was wrong. I was keeping weird hours,
eating very little and spending lots of time in my room;
I was constantly on edge and almost totally withdrawn
from my family. I know now that this time was really
hell for Mom. She knew I was using drugs, and it
really hurt her. I really admire her and the way she
handled the whole situation.

Sue's parents found her on drugs, and in their dec-
larations of love had made her a prisoner in her
home, and forced her to see a psychiatrist. In fact,
it was this constant pressure from her parents that
drove her further into the drugs. In contrast, my mother
never confronted me on the issue. She made a constant effort to show that she really loved me.

No matter how much I yelled at her and made fun
of her middle-class ideals and religion, she kept the
door open for me. I was often very cruel to her, trying to goad her into a fight. It would have been much
easier to justify my actions if I had the excuse that
she hated me, ignored me, or had thrown me out,
but she wouldn't be pushed into being my scapegoat.
She responded to my hostility with genuine love. She
never backed down from the things she believed in,
but she listened to me. She allowed me to make mistakes, always inviting me back with her invitations
to go places with her and the family, always inquiring
what I was doing, even though the answer was often,
"Mind your own business." She made every effort

to be loving, kind and understanding.

Her actions, rather than pushing me farther out and into the drug people to find consolation for my problems, invited me back to genuine love. I really believe that it was this unselfish love that helped me and made it worthwhile for me to suffer the pains of coming off, and the pain of admitting I had been wrong and needed help.

I don't live in my home town anymore. I've gone back several times and have seen my friends. Sue has been in the hospital a couple of times and is now out and trying very hard. She's had a hard time because she's had to go it alone, separating herself from her friends who are on drugs, and from her own home because her family can't understand her. She has to fight it out alone. This is really the sad part about drugs. Often when a kid wants to get off he can't turn to his parents because they can't understand, or are too afraid to face it.

I was luckier than most. I didn't go so far into drugs that it was impossible for me to come back. My family faced the situation and handled it, rather than running scared. That is the reason I'm writing this: to let you know the feeling that a kid in this situation is facing; and, hopefully, to help you if you ever have to face this problem.

by Dr. and Mrs. Jack Willke

# 19. How We Really Teach Sex

**H**OW do we really educate our children about sex?

Dad walks into the house, tired from a full day of work. The children cluster about him, greeting him happily. His wife, as happy to see him as he is her, shares a greeting kiss and warm embrace until they are interrupted by the little people trying to get between them for their little share of loving. The children have seen this often and are very aware that Mom and Dad love each other and that they enjoy this kissing business. Sex education? It most certainly is! And effective, healthy, well-balanced teaching too. This example of husband-wife love and joyful expression of it is what they will know marriage to be, and they very likely will be able to create a similar stable, loving home of their own someday because of this kind of teaching.

Sad to say — other less healthy examples teach children too. Let's watch:

Mother reluctantly picks up the baby and with obvious distaste does what must be done as she removes and cleans a particularly soiled and smelly diaper. The other children watch her obvious disgust at the whole dirty mess. Later, the word "dirty" during toilet training becomes more closely identified with the child's bottom. Sex education? Yes, this is too. One little building block in attitude formation that these children will carry the rest of their lives; one little training session toward associating genital organs (and ultimately their sexual use even in marriage) with dirtiness and, therefore, badness.

———————

Within earshot of the children after supper, Dad just has to tell Mom the very funny story about one of the salesmen and the affair he's having with the receptionist. "And you know, his wife doesn't suspect a thing." Both Mom and Dad get a good laugh. The children listen. They have been told of the sanctity of marriage? Certainly they have in school, in church, and, yes, even by these parents. But all of this remains just words, and words, and meaningless words. They now know what Mother and Dad really think and feel about marriage and fidelity from the real laughter from relating the story of extramarital playing around.

———————

Mother walks into her first-grade boy's bedroom to find him busily engaged rubbing his penis. She flares in frightened horror, scolds him with an emotional vehemence, warns him never, never, to do that again or he'll hurt himself, or even says that if he doesn't quit it, she'll have to take him to the doctor and have it cut off. This is sex education too, and in a very harmful way.

These last three examples are what we would call negative sex education. As you notice, none of these involves the direct teaching of facts of life, but nevertheless all do teach about sex and in a most impressive and lasting fashion. What about the dreaded sixty-four-dollar question? It might come like this. A report comes back from school that third-grade Johnny has been overheard using a certain four-letter word and will the parents please take care of this.

"Johnny, I hear that you got into some trouble in school this noon."

"Yeah, Dad, I don't know what they got excited about. Joe Case uses that word all the time."

"What did you say, John?"

"I just called him a 'fucker.' "

"Do you know what that word means, John?"

"Well, not exactly, I guess."

"Well, let me explain it to you. John, you know how much your Mother and Dad love each other, don't you?"

"Yeah."

"You know what a kiss is? It's a way of saying 'I love you,' maybe a little more than just words would say. Right, John? If we want to say to someone else that we love them very, very much then we might hug them very tightly. We do that with you sometimes, don't we?"

"Yep."

"Well, God has given to husbands and wives a very special and important way of showing their love for each other. Sometimes at night when a Mother and Dad love each other very much, they snuggle together and hug each other very tightly, so tightly that the father's penis goes between the mother's legs and right into her vagina. Did you know that, John?"

"You mean parents do that?"

"Yes, God has made this way of showing love, blessed it, and made it very holy, but he only wants a loving husband and wife to do this and use it as a way of saying how much they love each other."

"Ohhhhh, now, Mom told me something about that. That's how babies start, isn't it?"

"That's right, John, because some seed from the daddy's penis goes into the mother's body and then, if God wills, a new baby starts to grow, and, you see, that baby then comes because the mother and dad love each other so much."

"Oh, I see. But what's that got to do with teacher's note?"

"Well, you see, John, the word 'fuck' is a slang or a bad word for this act of loving. Only ignorant and dumb kids use it. It's not a nice word and you should never use it, because it's a vulgar way of talking about something that is so wonderful, good, and holy. We should only use good words and be respectful when we talk about it. So if you see that word written on the wall of a boy's bathroom or on a fence or a playground you'll know enough not to use it."

Compare the above with what would have been planted in some little mind and heart if Dad would have ducked or punished, and refused to discuss it, except to forbid him to use that "dirty" word. Let's look at one more good example.

At suppertime Dad, the children, and Mother are eating. It so happens that the youngest child is eating too, snuggled against his Mommy, nursing busily, when, unannounced, into the room walk Mr. and Mrs. Jones and little Andy from next door. Modestly covered as she is with her pull-up sweater and trapdoor bra, the young mother does not interrupt the baby's meal, but comfortably and easily greets the neighbors, showing neither embarrassment nor upset.

Without a word being spoken, a very positive lesson indeed has been given these children in teaching them that breast feeding is a natural, normal part of life, and in this atmosphere they will grow up without the prudishness, half guilt, and half shame about this and other normal body functions that too many of our adults possess.

What sort of attitudes prevail at your house? Sex education isn't always so much what's said, it's often

what is not said. Children don't always listen to the
words we say, but they usually do notice how comfortable or uncomfortable, how upset, how happy, or
otherwise we are. Children grow up ultimately to do
what they saw us do and to become largely what we
were. Certainly they listen to what we say, but when
they become old enough to make their own decisions,
they tend to act out their lives much in the way that
they saw us act out ours. Few of us realize that most
of the sex education that a child is ever going to get
has been gotten and solidly planted in their minds
and hearts before they ever start school. Their total
concept of manhood and womanhood, of maleness and
femaleness, of what a husband and wife are and
should be, of what marriage is — all of this is learned
in their preschool years; all of this is learned as they
read the book of our lives.

It's interesting to read the literal barrage of articles
in the popular press on the subject of sex education,
all of which seem to us to have several common denom-
inators. They all take for granted that sex has not
been adequately taught at home, and they assume
that parents are, by and large, incompetent to give
this instruction. The general conclusion is that therefore the schools must do so. We speak to thousands of
parents every year and find that many of them are
quite offended by thus being written off. Most parents,
we find, are sincere about wanting to do this job for
their children themselves . . . and doing it adequately.
Whichever attitude we take, however, we should realize that a fact of life is that, like it or not, parents *are*
the primary sex educators. As long as parents raise
children in homes this will continue to be so for better
or for worse. Our primary job must first of all be to
help parents do the job that only they do so completely in those preschool years and on upwards as
the child matures.

We must impress on parents that, as the examples
above show, most sex education is very informal in-

deed. Most of it is on the spur of the moment and meeting the need as it arises. Some of it is accomplished without saying a word. Facts of life are important and parents should be giving this information very early and adequately, but *how* they give these facts is usually more important than the facts themselves. The really important thing is their attitudes . . . how Mom and Dad feel about this.

One final word as to the place of school and teacher. Just as sex education at home is only as good as the parents, and how they feel about sex, so any sex education that we put in school will be only as good and every bit as bad as the teacher. It will reflect the balance of healthy sexuality, the reverence and joy of this man or woman, or it will also teach their rigidity, frigidity, prudishness, upset, fears, and prejudices. Yes, we do need more biological facts of life taught in school and we need them taught earlier, but long before the student, even in the most "enlightened" school, will get these facts in a classroom, he will have been hearing them on the street corner and, yes, even in the sandbox. Most sex education in school, as most at home, comes at the informal moment, the natural teaching opportunity, the little question answered by the teacher, a reaction to the picture drawn on the blackboard when she walks into the room, her attitudes. Health and biology classes later merely add details to basic facts long since known, and reinforce moral values already experienced as a norm.

Yes, we need sex education in our schools — a lot more than we're getting. But while we are busy thinking of inserting it into the curriculum, let us be many times busier helping to form in our parents and our teachers a well-balanced concept of sexuality, because on this subject, probably more than any other, little people learn from big people's lives. Let's help to form these big people, so that their lives will teach constructively.